WALNEY ISLAND GIRL

WALNEY ISLAND GIRL

KATIE PERCY

Katie at her sister Evelyn's wedding.

First published 2011
Reprinted 2020

The History Press
97 St George's Place, Cheltenham,
Gloucestershire, GL50 3qb
www.thehistorypress.co.uk

British Library Cataloguing in Publication Data.
A catalogue record for this book is available from the British Library.

ISBN 978 0 7509 5115 9

Typesetting and origination by The History Press
Printed in Great Britain by TJ International Ltd, Padstow, Cornwall.

CONTENTS

1   My Early Memories   7

2   Family Pride   16

3   A Trip to Liverpool   24

4   A Free Lunch   31

5   I Become an Avid Reader   39

6   A Visit to Maud's   46

7   Family Loss   57

8   Hospital   64

9   Clogs   68

10 School and Friends   74

11 A Guide at Last!   81

12 Off to the Lakes   88

13 The Queen's at Biggar   95

14 Katie's War and the Steel Girls' Strike   113

15 A New Life   123

Chapter One

MY EARLY MEMORIES

I was born in Barrow-in-Furness in December 1920, and was Christened Kathleen, a name I disliked. I hated the shortened versions even more. To me Kathy sounded 'soppy', while 'Kaff' I detested. This silly 'name' sounded like 'chaff', a hollow, empty husk with no substance. I felt there was more to me than that. I much preferred Kate or Katie.

There is some dispute about when memory actually begins, but my earliest memory was of a huge upheaval when I was about three years old. We were moving from Barrow to Walney Island. This experience and those following became indelibly printed on my mind – some of them came back to haunt me many times throughout my life.

This move seemed to be a tremendous journey, in pouring rain. The weather was very cold and I remember feeling frightened. We were in a caravan which was being pulled along by an enormous horse, a Shire. I could see the horse's broad back and its strong, rippling muscles, which were glistening with rain. A man walked beside the horse holding its halter, and my Dad walked alongside.

They were hard times. My Dad, William Edward Percy, who was born in Widnes, served in the Regular Army but was too old to go to France. In 1916 he was invalided out of the Army because of an injury to his leg caused by an accident with an officer's horse. Thereafter, he walked with a limp.

However, he was directed to Barrow to work on munitions, where by the hand of fate, he met my mother who had been brought over from Galway, Ireland, also for war work. They had begun their life together in shabby rooms, because there was a severe housing shortage in Barrow, due to the hundreds who had rushed in from other areas to take up munitions work in Vickers Shipyard, as well as Barrow Steelworks.

Vickers had enjoyed the boom years of the First World War, during which they employed thousands of people. But after the Armistice in 1918 they began laying them off. The women, including my mother, were the first to go. My father, who was laid off in 1919, was forced to join the dole queue along with thousands of others. My brother William was born in October 1919, myself in December 1920, and younger brother Leslie at the end of July 1922. Conditions in the lodging-house were very overcrowded, so Dad began the heartbreaking task of looking for somewhere to live. All he could find was a caravan in a builder's yard which he'd 'bought for a song', or so he had told our mother. Next he travelled out of town to nearby Walney Island searching for a piece of land on which to site the caravan. In this problem, luck was on his side. A landowner on the island agreed to lease him a portion of a field for a small yearly rent, and that is where my life really began.

Outside our dingy lodgings in Barrow, Dad piled our meagre possessions into the caravan, while our mother anxiously climbed in, carrying Les, hustling Will and me up the step, and closed the door behind her. Dad walked alongside the owner of the heavy Shire horse. The journey of 2 miles took us out of the town, across Michaelson Road Bridge to Barrow Island and some tenement flats which overlooked the Vickers works. We passed by their engineering sheds, turned towards Walney Bridge, and crossed over. Next the road turned left going uphill along the promenade which faced the channel and the shipyard, then went downhill along Ocean Road before turning into Carr Lane, passing a row of elegant houses, known as Beach Crescent.

The lane ran alongside a dark green marsh, pitted with the gullies created by the force of the tides of the Irish Sea surging into the channel. Walney Channel itself was a mere strip of pewter-grey water lapping dismally at the base of the shipbuilding stocks of the distant Vickers shipyard and its dock walls. Further along the marsh a significant landmark built on a pile of rocks was Walney Lighthouse. On the other side of the lane stretched a patchwork of green fields misted with rain, owned by the farmers in the nearby Biggar Village. Opposite one of these fields the farmer finally brought his horse and its burden to a standstill.

Katie's father, William Edward Percy, in his Army days.

Immediately Mam jumped up from her seat, opened the top half of the caravan door and stared out through the rain at her surroundings. Will and I followed and stood at each side of her, clinging to her dark skirt. Les was asleep.

Dad opened the gate and the farmer coaxed the Shire into the sodden field, which, under its weight and the burden of the caravan, soon became a quagmire. The big animal slipped and slithered and snorted furiously, blowing clouds of steam as he exerted and struggled to place his huge, heavily shod hooves on to the slushy surface, trying to move forward. They were barely inside the gate, when the horse became stuck. The impatient farmer called out,

'That's as far as my poor horse can go in this weather!'

'You'll get no money out of me if you leave me stuck here!' Dad threatened.

They stood glaring at each other while the poor horse seemed to be slowly sinking into the mud. By my side, my mother became alarmed. She shouted,

'Tell him I want to be farther back! Not dumped inside the gate!'

'You heard what my wife said! If you don't get your horse moving, I will!'

Dad moved purposefully towards the animal, but the burly farmer held up a warning hand.

'You keep away from him!'

Trembling with cold and anxiety, I stared wide-eyed at the big, whinnying horse and listened with fear to the angry exchange of voices across the lonely field. Exasperated, the angry farmer began coaxing his horse once again. Finally, inch by slow inch, the horse, exerting itself and snorting in distress, began moving. The farmer coaxed him to turn, back up, and turn again. Finally, Dad gave the farmer a curt nod.

'Here will have to do.'

He handed him some coins.

Cursing at my Dad, the farmer pocketed the money and began to untether his horse's harness from out of the caravan shafts, and slipping and sliding in the mud, led him away through the gate into the lane that led to the village. And so began our caravan life in an open field facing the marshy gullies. Beyond those lay the distant iron forest of shipyard cranes, belonging to the mighty Vickers shipyard.

The caravan, in spite of the faded and peeling pink paint on the outside, was quite attractive within, and had once been the pride and joy of a travelling showman, perhaps part of a fair. The inside was lined with polished walnut panels on the walls, the space divided into two rooms and partitioned with a sliding door that hid the bedroom where we three children would share a big double bed. Set in this dividing wall was a small open fireplace with a tiled surround and hearth, and above, a mantelpiece of polished walnut. This had a fancy mirror with little side-brackets for knick-knacks, which Mam loved. The rest was living space with a huge polished cupboard at the other end, which when opened revealed a double bed that folded down for our parents. The floor was covered in red patterned lino, and there was a small folding table and some padded seats.

Dad was immensely pleased to have found the caravan and a place to live that was his own, the only drawback being that there was no water laid on, though there was a standpipe at the top of the field from which water could be drawn. He was especially pleased with the land around the caravan and could see its potential. A vegetable garden, a few hens, a goat perhaps. The dole was a miserly amount, but he had a small Army disability pension of a pound a week which he hoped to use for what he had in mind.

Unfortunately for Dad none of these plans could be brought to fruition as soon as he wanted. The section of the lane where we lived, facing the gullies, was subject to flooding during the spring tides. The council had already begun to raise the level of the lane at the junction of Ocean Road and Carr Lane, to prevent the sea water reaching the houses at the lower end of Beach Crescent. They tipped many truckloads of rubble and household rubbish which they covered with black gravel, thus creating a mound that sloped gradually down to Carr Lane from the last house on the Crescent.

The family who lived in this end house were called the Mortons. Mr Morton and his son Alfred worked in the shipyard offices. The front of the house contained a shop selling groceries and sweets and was

The stocks at Biggar Village.

managed by Mrs Morton and her daughter Madge. Later on, when we were older and going to school, Mam, if she had a shilling or two left out of the dole, would sometimes send us down the lane for a loaf or a packet of salt or sugar from Mrs Morton's shop. We were always fascinated by the rows of sweet jars on one side of the counter; coconut teacakes, caramels, gobstoppers, aniseed balls, liquorice sticks and liquorice allsorts, lollipops, and little packets of sweet powder with a small stick of liquorice called Kali. We would stare longingly at the jars, for we had no money to buy sweets.

But if pretty Madge, Mrs Morton's daughter was serving, she seemed to take pity on us. Her warm brown eyes would fix on our yearning faces for a moment, crinkling, and her mouth smiling. Then teasing us, her hand would hover over the jars in turn. 'This one?' she would ask.

Along the Walney coastline today.

Finally she stopped over the caramel jar, unscrewed the lid, and brought out three caramels which, with a mischievous giggle, she dropped one by one into our eagerly awaiting hands. We thanked her, put Mam's grocery items in the bass bag (a cheap bag made of raffia) and left the shop with the sweets already in our mouths. This piece of toffee was wrapped in a neat square of patterned paper which we twisted into various shapes while we were slowly savouring the buttery sweet, as we slid down the gravel slope of the tip to Carr Lane and made our way home. The Mortons were a lovely family, especially Madge, and we loved going to their shop.

Whether the council ever intended to raise the rest of the lane, no-one knew. Every spring Carr Lane continued to flood, the salt water flowing over the marsh and across the lane into the fields. The lower part of one of these was where Dad had hoped to create a garden. The lane would have been better-named 'Tide's Reach Lane'! Farther south along the lane there was a medieval dyke which stretched as far as Biggar Village. It had been constructed by the monks of Furness Abbey in ancient times to protect the village and inhabitants from the invading tides. In turn, down the centuries the villagers followed the laws designated by the monks to keep the dyke in good repair.

Dad must have been horrified by the sight of sea water flooding his newly dug patch of earth. But never one to be daunted by obstacles, he approached the landowner, requesting we should be allowed to move to another field farther along the lane towards Biggar Village that was protected by the ancient dyke. The man, who had other fields, readily agreed, and in a few days, thanks to him, the caravan was settled on a new site. It was moved there by a different farmer, to a higher field further along the lane, protected by the dyke, this time with less trouble and in fine spring-like weather. Dad began once again clearing stubbly grass, and turning over the soil ready for planting. Fortunately, the soil was in very good heart, having been well-cultivated when growing crops, before being set aside and left as meadow.

The sights and sounds around us were what gave me my first awareness of my surroundings. Sitting down on rough clumps of grass for the first time, I shivered as the green spears scratched against my bare legs and hands, but felt comforted by Mam sitting beside me with Les on her lap. I enjoyed seeing the spring sunshine glinting on her head and loved the bronze highlights in her thick auburn hair, and the glorious way that the hair rippled in deep waves down to her waist.

We watched Dad with his spade, steadily digging, and turning over the earth, in this renewed effort to turn a part of another rough field into friable soil for a productive garden. Will stood alongside, watching. Spotting a soil-encrusted wriggling worm, he stooped quickly, picked up the worm, then dropped it again, while nearby a vigilant robin swooped across and bore the hapless worm swiftly away. I became aware of the smell of the cows in the next field, and heard the mournful cry of a curlew in the distance.

Flying from the marshes, flocks of seagulls soared and swooped filling the air with their raucous screeching calls as they sped overhead in a white cloud of movement, to the nearby shore of the Irish Sea at Biggar Bank. This then, was to be our place, our familiar environment in which we were to grow up. Dad often joked about it. He said 'Barrow was the last place God made, and Walney just fell off the end of his shovel.' There was nothing beautiful or picturesque to be seen in the bleakness of winter, but in the summer the salt marsh had a beauty of its own. The sameness of the harsh grass was enhanced by a carpet of sea pinks which covered the entire marsh right to the road edge. Dad seemed to like living there. He was in his own place, with lots of plans in his mind.

Walney Island is about 10 miles long and 2 miles wide. Thin, curving, this narrow stretch of land had been beaten into the shape of a coathanger by the surging tides of the Irish Sea. These tides swept in at the north and south ends of the island joining the narrow waters of Walney Channel, flooding across the salt marsh, filling the gullies and during the spring tides overflowing on to the lane and fields. There were two villages, North Scale at the north end, and Biggar, nearer to the south end of the island where there was a coastguard station. The island faced the small town of Barrow-in-Furness where the main employer was the giant Vickers-Armstrong Shipbuilding Works, which depended on the channel for the launching of their ships. There was also a much smaller firm, the Barrow Haematite Steel Company at the north end of the town.

Chapter Two

FAMILY PRIDE

Our pre-school years of living in that rather bleak place were happy. Like all innocent children we were unaware of our poverty and of our parents' struggle for survival. The three of us, Will, Les and I, ragged and barefoot, played all day in summer running around in that field, collecting daisies, and dandelion 'clocks', laughing as we blew their gossamer seeds to the wind. We even ventured onto the marsh, sitting down in one of the gullies making mud pies and what we called 'darba-la-las' – long strips of mud rolled in our hands like snakes. But we always heeded Dad's warning to watch out for the tides. As soon as we saw water creeping in to the gully we were off, running back across the marsh to the safety of our own place behind the dyke.

Sometimes we ventured farther up the field where a couple lived in a wooden bungalow and had a small garden, and there was a piggery a little farther away. The man called Johnnie Crabtree looked after the pigs for his mother, Mrs Crabtree, who lived in a comfortable brick house on Ocean Road. She was a sturdy little woman who often chatted to Dad in his garden and became friendly with our Mam visiting her whenever she had a new baby.

Once, when one of the pigs had a litter, Mrs Crabtree, the owner, invited Mam to go along to see them. Mam wrapped her baby son in a knitted shawl and made her way through the rough field, with us three trailing behind her to the smelly dark sheds that were the piggery. We all stood beside Mam gazing over the low wall at a huge pig that was lying stretched out on the straw. Beside her were a row of small wriggling piglets suckling on her fat belly. To me they looked like fat rolls of pink bacon. Mam exclaimed in wonder at the sight of them and congratulated Mrs Crabtree.

'My word, missus, don't they look fine and healthy!'

Mrs Crabtree, whose red, lined face looked like a withered apple, nodded as proudly as though she had given birth to them herself. She picked up a piglet which squealed in protest at being removed from its breakfast. Turning to my mother, Mrs Crabtree grinned, glanced at us and said with a voice full of meaning, 'This is the sort of stock you want, Mary!' Mam, not in the least offended by her little brood being compared to a litter of pigs, laughed merrily. She was proud of her little family, and doted on her boys.

She giggled about Mrs Crabtree's remark all the way down the field. She was a lot of fun when we were small, and had a streak of mischief. We used to laugh at the way she acted coy and girlish whenever Tim, an Irish ex-sailor, now a coastguard stationed at the coastguard station at the south end of Walney, stopped by our gate. Once a month on a Friday, was the day he picked up his salary in town. Mam always knew what time he would return. From the window she would watch him rolling unsteadily along the lane uniform cap askew, ripe and red-faced from the whisky he had imbibed in his favourite watering hole in town.

Quickly, she would hustle us down the path as soon as he drew level with our gate knowing he would stop at the sight of her children. Then she herself would sashay down to the gate, glorious hair flowing over her shoulders, blue Irish eyes smiling coquettishly. No matter what the time of day, Tim would be full of blarney and booze exclaiming,

'Top o' the morning to ye, my lovely colleen.' Swaying unsteadily over the gate he would thrust his hand into his pocket and bring out some small change which he would drop into our eagerly expectant hands. And he always asked the same question . . .

'Is this all your tribe, Mary mavourneen?'

He would reach up with a freckled hand and fondle his ginger beard as he gazed down at us affectionately with bleary bloodshot eyes, and Mam would giggle girlishly as the blarney flowed between them. We liked him, thought of him as a kind uncle who always gave us something. Then, probably half asleep, and longing to put his head

Katie's mother Mary O'Flaherty in later life.

down Tim would stumble away along the lane on his long trek back to the coastguard station. Dad who had gone into town to sign on, knew nothing about these little encounters, and would probably have laughed anyway, and dismissed Tim as a silly old bugger who drank more than was good for him.

There was no harm in Mam – to her it was just a giggle. There was also method in her madness. When we went back indoors she quickly collected from us the threepenny bits or sixpences that Tim had given us and repaid us with a penny each for us to spend at Morton's shop. We were too young to know the value of the coins anyway. To Mam this money went into her secret little hoard for forays into town amid the second-hand stalls. She enjoyed 'rooting' for clothes for us and Dad too. His smart one and only outfit was of excellent quality, she had a good eye for a bargain, and would put it by with the stallholder and pay a bit off the balance each week until she was able to carry it home in triumph.

When unemployment in Barrow deepened into the Depression, more poor people arrived on the top Bank Road, bringing pitiful little huts, caravans and a railway carriage or two, to live in, facing the restless Irish Sea. Most of them had been evicted for failing to pay their rent. One poor family had only a large bell-tent. All these children ran around the fields and the cobbled beach at Biggar Bank like us, and in time we all went to the same school at Ocean Road just over a mile away, as did the children from Biggar Village, almost a mile south of where we lived.

The man who lived in the bell-tent walked on a wooden stump after losing part of his leg in the First World War. He and his wife had been evicted from their rented house, and lived with their three sons – how they managed to keep warm in Walney Island's bleak winters, I have no idea. But Mam often spoke of how cold the mother always looked, her poor red nose constantly dripping.

About four other families moved onto the upper part of the field where we lived. Although poor, because the husband was out of work, these families were very decent, clean-living people. Later on, when we were older and attending school, we became friends with the two little girls of the Albion family. We were often invited into their home, a former railway carriage. Inside, it was impeccably clean. The small Dover stove shone from frequent black-leading, and even the metal chimney that went up through the roof shone like patent leather. A colourful pegged, rag-rug covered the floor in front of the stove. Their modest pieces of furniture and chairs were also well-cared for, and the small net curtains on the windows were crisp and white. This family had obviously been used to a comfortable well-kept home and had fallen on hard times. We used to enjoy a game of dominoes, or cards around their table. Mostly it was Will who was invited, as I was often minding one of my siblings.

They seemed especially fond of Will, perhaps because they only had two little girls, Irene and Edna. Irene was about my age and was in my class at school. Edna was a couple of years younger.

Their home seemed a very pleasant and happy household. Mr Albion helped his wife by shaking the mats and cleaning the small windows. He only had a small patch of garden in which he grew a few potatoes and cabbages. Mostly he went to the market to buy much of the family's food, bringing back two bags full on dole day as well as on other days. My Dad was very lucky in being able to rent such a large portion of the lower field, and create a splendid garden, and have poultry. The other families, who lived farther up the field, had to pass our place in order to reach the lane. Some used to stop to admire Dad's wonderful garden. They were probably envious as well.

Will admired the Albion family very much. After visiting them he would tell Mam how cosy and clean their place was. Mam used to get really irritated, muttering to herself that 'they only had two kids to clean up after.' I think she was just jealous her eldest son chose to spend his time with them, instead of at home. Irene and Edna were never allowed to run wild on Biggar Bank as we were. They spent their evenings reading, knitting, or doing cork-work. Will said the whole family were always doing something.

A little farther along the field was another family. Their abode could only be described as a box on wheels. The door was reached by climbing about six wooden steps. Their eldest child, a white-faced, thin girl called Mona who was in my class at school, took me inside the hut one day when her parents were out. Inside there was only one room which contained one large bed upon which they all slept. They had three children and were the poorest of the poor, but were kind, gentle people, evicted from their rented house when the father lost his teaching job

There didn't appear to be any sort of cupboard in the hut. Mona reached under one of the pillows and brought out a loaf. Stooping, she reached under the bed and brought out a plate and a knife, some Stork margarine, and began cutting off a slice of bread. She offered me a slice also, but I declined politely, saying my dinner would be ready. The thought of people having to keep bread under the pillow nauseated me.

We were poor but this family had nothing. Nothing at all. Mona's Dad was tall, thin and pale, and spoke in a refined, educated way, with a slightly Welsh accent. He suffered with chest trouble, and probably lacked the energy to dig up the long grass around the hut in order to grow vegetables.

Sometimes, Mona's mother, an older version of herself, would invite me inside their humble home. Even though they had very little for themselves, she was very hospitable. She would make a simple kind of Welsh Rarebit, by melting cheese in a pan on the tiny stove, and pouring it over slices of bread, to which she would add a sprinkling of pepper, then offer me a slice. This appeared to be what they lived on. This poor family all looked like cheese themselves.

Higher along the field from this family was a little caravan owned by a homely Scottish couple who had no children, so they must have had a far better existence than the couples with children. They seemed to like our family, and would come down the field to chat to Dad in the garden, and perhaps buy a cauliflower, or a cabbage. The wife would always call my brother Willie, which he hated. With her pronounced Scottish accent it came out like 'Worllie' which used to make us titter and we would tease Will about it. The husband, Isaac, who seemed a bit furtive, was known by everybody as Ikey. We often saw him raking about on the Biggar Bank shore at night if the tide was receding. I learned a few years later, that he used to set lobster pots to catch lobsters, which was against the law, as this required a licence. Ikey supplemented his dole by selling the lobsters, or crabs, if he caught any, to the proprietor who managed the Queen's Arms pub in Biggar Village.

Looking back over my life now, the poverty and squalor in which people were forced to live in those days appals me. In the 1920s at school, we were learning about the British Empire. I was bewildered in my early years, and at a loss to understand why, if Britain was so rich and powerful, with the greatest Empire the world had ever known, her 'sons' should be without jobs. They had fought an unnecessary and diabolical war against Germany, in which millions had been killed. Those who survived suffered the loss of limbs, eyesight, or had been gassed. In 1918 the British government had promised the soldiers would be returning 'to

William, Katie's father.

a land fit for heroes to live in', and houses would be built. Thousands of returning servicemen found there were no jobs to go to, and no houses to live in. Men who had lost their limbs suffered the indignity of having to sit in a wooden box on main streets selling matches to passers-by.

Empire Day was celebrated on 24 May when we were given a half-day's holiday. At lunchtime we would be gathered in the school hall and have to sing the 'Empire Day' song. This began 'Pride of Empire and of country' – etc, etc. How could children growing up in poverty feel proud of an empire they could not even envisage? What had the Empire given to them? Their fathers were out of work, they had no decent clothes or shoes to wear, and a lot of them were going home to a shack to eat bread and margarine. To them 'Pride of Empire' and 'Pride of country' were meaningless, empty words. Those who had gained from the overseas 'possessions' were the rich and the aristocracy. Later, when I was older and read more, I never felt pride in the Empire. All I felt was shame. Empire to me meant the subjugation of peoples, and the plundering of their countries' wealth, whether it be gold, diamonds, rubber, or tea and coffee, by rich speculators from Britain, Holland, Germany and America.

Chapter Three

A TRIP TO LIVERPOOL

The children living in the huts were our friends. The children from Biggar Village were not. They looked down their noses at us. Passing down the lane on their way to school, these children stuck their tongues out, calling us gypsies as we stood at the gate in our bare feet. When we began at school we understood how insulting this name-calling was meant to be. Most of them were farmers' children and considerably better off than we were. To be poor was to be despised. We were the ragged Percy family who lived in a caravan, therefore were gypsies. In those days gypsies were perceived as thieves who lived on their wits. The village girls told other girls at school about where we lived. Therefore I was taunted with this insult, as well as 'Percy pig' during all my school years.

Village women passing on their way to shop at nearby Vickerstown stared in curiosity at the man who laboured constantly in his garden, and at the shabby-looking caravan where poorly-dressed children played outside. One or two women who were not farmers' wives, were friendly, and would stop to chat to Mam if she was near the gate with us. One of them, whom we came to know as Maud, was invited by Mam into our caravan and soon became a regular visitor, usually staying all afternoon gossiping avidly about the village people, and drinking tea with Mam. Maud was an 'incomer', an outsider, who only lived at Biggar because her husband did a bit of casual work in the village. They had no history of 'belonging' there and were only tolerated by these insular villagers, who all seemed to be related by blood and marriage.

In the first couple of years after moving into the field, Dad was busy from morning to night working in all weathers, which imposed a great strain on his health. His old Army injury was troubling him, as well as arthritis in his joints. The doctor advised him to return to the military hospital in Liverpool where he had had the injury treated.

Though Dad hated having to go away from us all, leaving a lot of his work unfinished, he had to comply with doctor's orders because of his Army pension. However, he was able to arrange some lodgings in Liverpool so that Mam and we children could be there too. I was about four years old at the time. I remember the train journey as uneventful, but the arrival at the lodgings was more exciting. There were some lovely parks with lakes nearby, where Mam would take us to feed the ducks with bits of bread the landlady, Mrs Watson, gave us. Sometimes Mam would go out to visit Dad taking Les with her, but leaving Will and I behind and cautioning us to behave ourselves and not bother the landlady.

But sometimes the landlady would be out too and we would be left to our own devices. Five-year-old Will, always the mischievous one, would begin to explore with me following behind. We crept on our hands and knees across the landing and found the other doors were unlocked. There were some curious things to examine in Mrs Watson's rooms. I was fascinated with a glass dish that had pink and white things like crabs crouching in the water. Mam told me later on that they were Mrs Watson's false teeth.

There were various little boxes on her dressing-table which we opened to find odd bits of jewellery and many coloured beads that must have belonged to broken necklaces. Will picked out two bright red ones and stuck one up each nostril and two more in each ear, and began whooping like a thing possessed. I did the same, pushing green beads up my nostrils and copying Will. We had great fun until we heard Mam's voice calling for us. Hastily we pulled the beads out and put them back in the box. Unfortunately for me, I couldn't get one of them out of my nostril. I must have pushed the bead up too far.

Mam was absolutely furious with us for going into Mrs Watson's rooms and for pushing beads up our nostrils. She tried in vain to remove the green one, even at one point using a button-hook. In the end she had to get us all ready to go to the hospital casualty department, a

Katie's mother Mary on Walney Beach in later life.

frightening place for a four-year-old like me, but luckily the doctor had the right instrument and quickly removed the bloodstained bead. That was my strongest memory of Liverpool.

The rest and treatment at the military hospital in Liverpool must have done Dad a lot of good. In no time he was busy as ever trying to catch up with the jobs he had left unfinished. Will had been going to school for a year, now it was my turn to start. Back in his stride, Dad had worked wonders with his portion of field, which because of a regular rainfall, was always slushy. Mam, driven mad by us running in and out bringing mud in on our feet, nagged him about paths, so Dad bought a load of broken paving slabs that were going cheap. He laid an attractive crazy paving path running from the front of the caravan to the gate, as well as laying some slabs around the sides and back.

On each side of this attractive path at the front, working from early morning to dusk, he had gradually created a huge vegetable garden. There was row upon neat row of cabbages, carrots, potatoes, swedes, turnips, lettuces, radishes, peas and beans, as well as parsnips and sprouts. He even left some space for summer flowers to border the path. He also erected a trellis screen to hide the caravan from the inquisitive eyes of passers-by, and on it grew climbing roses and sweet-peas.

Dad had always planned to build on to the caravan at the back. He was well aware how hard life was for Mam. She complained constantly about the lack of space with no amenities for washing and cooking. She had struggled for years with only that one small grate which took one pan on its tiny hob. We had survived on pans of stew or soup, but how she had managed, I have no idea. This small fireplace was in constant use and was a fire hazard.

Once when Dad had gone to collect his dole, Mam had a big pot of stew boiling on its small hob. She was standing outside busily washing the family's clothes, labouring over a tin bath mounted on two trestles when she heard an awful roaring noise. Looking up from her task she was horrified when she saw that the long black chimney had overheated and black smoke was pouring out. Alerted at once to the danger she rushed into the caravan with a bucket of water. We were playing marbles on the floor unaware there was anything wrong, until she screamed at us.

'Quick! Get outside!'

Unbeknown to us the cupboards behind the fireplace near our bed were in danger of becoming alight until Mam doused the glowing coals, which also put out the fire. Fortunately the iron pan sitting on the hob had a sturdy lid, so the stew was unharmed. If she had failed to act so coolly and promptly, the whole caravan would have been set alight and we would have been made homeless and perhaps even burned to death. She was very upset by what could have happened and rushed to tell Dad as soon as he arrived.

'Oh! Bill! Something awful happened! I don't know what I would have done if the children had been hurt.'

She dashed the tears away and told him what had taken place.

He looked astonished and his face paled. He put a comforting arm around her shaking shoulders, and praised her prompt action.

'You were very cool, Mary, acting so quickly!'

Later inside the caravan he inspected the doused fire, and frowned when he saw the stack of half-burnt coal.

'You should never pile the coal so high up, Mary! The chimney gets too hot, and it doesn't take much to set wooden cupboards alight!'

Poor Mam! Her face reddened and she bit her lip.

'So it was my fault! I'm sorry Bill! I'll be more careful in future!'

Over the years in between working in his garden, Dad had drawn out a rough outline for a large kitchen on a piece of lined paper. Now, seeing how upset Mam was, he brought out the plan from its hiding place in a small niche in the mantelpiece. Spreading the square of paper out on the small table, he showed her the plans to reassure her while we gathered around eagerly to watch and listen. We longed for more space as much as Mam did.

He tapped the paper with a work-scarred finger.

'See? There'll be a decent-sized kitchen and you'll have a grand cooking range big enough to take the iron kettle and three pans on its hob, so you'll never have to cook on that small fireplace again! Also, you'll have a scullery with a sink, and I'll bring the boiler in from outside, so you will be inside doing the washing. How does that sound, Mary?' he asked, eagerly.

He glanced from her to us, smiling.

'Can we call our caravan a bungalow then, Dad?' I asked hopefully. 'I'm fed up of the village kids calling us gypsies!'

Dad laughed.

'You can if you like. But take no notice of them, lass. If we are gypsies, those poor people in the tent further up the field must be Arabs! But we know they're not, don't we? They are like us with nowhere else to live that's all!'

Mam stared in concentration at the piece of paper, her face troubled. She was unable to see the kitchen he described in the pencilled lines and squares on the paper. Unconvinced, she was unable to share his enthusiasm and sighed in despair.

'I've waited all these years, struggling daily with only that small fire to cook meals. Then, today – '

She blinked hard and shuddered.

'It was so frightening to think what could have happened! I feel at the end of my tether!'

She pushed the sheet of paper aside dismissively.

'I can't see how this bit of paper is bringing my new kitchen any nearer, Bill!'

'But it is. It is!' Dad insisted, patting her hand. 'The materials are all ordered and partly paid for. I will be picking some of it up this week. Don't you worry, Mary! I will be starting on it soon!'

As well as planning for the kitchen and scullery, Dad had built a hen-hut, and a wired-in run for poultry to scratch about in. He had always wanted to have fresh eggs, to make up for the fact that the dole was only sufficient to provide basic groceries. Things like meat and butter were luxuries, so were eggs. But he had the initiative to realise he could at least, provide us with eggs.

But all this took time, and money. Dad was unemployed all the years of my childhood, but he was never idle. He made the most of what he had, which was the dole, and his pound a week disability pension from the Army. The dole was a miserable pittance, 7s 6d for himself, 5s for his wife, and 2s per head for each child. With this he had to feed us all. If that had been all we had to depend on we would have starved most of the time. The saving grace for us was his wonderful productive garden. Eight months of the year we lived on tasty potatoes and vegetables. By December the only produce left in the garden was a few potatoes and some sprouts.

Like all children we waited in anticipation for Christmas. There wasn't the money for toys, and only a hearty beef stew to eat. But after the kitchen was built and the good cooking range installed, our parents made sure our Christmas dinner was special. Dad would buy a roasting fowl from Barrow market. Later when he had his own poultry he would kill a hen or a duck. A bunch of sage would hang from the ceiling drying in readiness for the stuffing. Mam would chop the onions, rub the sage over them releasing a powerful aroma, add salt and pepper and make wonderful sage and onion stuffing to go into the fowl. We enjoyed standing near, watching them create a huge Christmas pudding. We would lick our lips in anticipation, as they measured in the lovely raisins and currants, candied peel, spices, suet, black treacle and flour. Mam would break up the candied peel and give us a bit each to suck while she diced the rest of it to add to the pudding. We loved this little treat, followed by a lucky stir of the dark spicy mass of the pudding. Then it would be piled into a greased, white cloth, tied up and put on to boil in a big iron pan, while we scraped eagerly around the sides of the big dish for any sticky bits remaining.

The Christmas meal was the dinner of the year, with succulent chicken or duck, sprouts, carrots, potatoes, mouth-watering gravy, and that rich pudding to follow smothered in white sauce. After Christmas there was always some Christmas pudding left. So Mam would cut some off, fry it, and we would set off for school with a huge slice to tuck in to. But afterwards in the New Year we often went hungry. Winter was a cruel time for us.

Chapter Four

A FREE LUNCH

Walney Island was cold and bleak with freezing rain blowing across the marsh, and a gusting wind blowing down the field from across the Irish Sea, so we got the bad weather from both sides. We dreaded going to bed as it took us ages to get warm under the old Army blankets. Mam would pile our coats on the top of our bed to add weight and more warmth. The caravan walls were not insulated against cold weather, or noise. We would lie there listening to the constant hammering from the shipyard which seemed to be louder at night, as well as the noise from the channel dredgers.

There was the regular clump and crash of their buckets as they dug down into the water to collect silt and debris brought in by the tides from the Irish Sea. Then the clanging of metal chains as they brought the buckets up again to deposit the silt and rubbish into the hold of the boat. This was an important job as they had to keep the channel clear and deep enough to enable Vickers to launch their newly built ships.

Later on when Dad had completed the kitchen and added the cooking range, he would bank the fire up at night with cinders and a shovel of coke to keep it going all night. He would also put some house bricks in the oven to warm up, and put them in the bed. This helped a lot but we often banged our toes against them if the bit of blanket in which they were wrapped got loose. Some nights he would also put the oven shelves in our bed before we got undressed and climbed in. This helped us to keep warm and get off to sleep.

For the first three months of the year the ground was rock hard, frozen in winter's merciless grip. The barrels which Dad had placed at each corner of the van to catch rain water were covered in a thick layer of ice. In the mornings getting ready for school, we had to take an enamel dish and bash the ice in order to get enough water to have a wash. We shivered, unwilling to plunge our hands into that freezing water. Instead we settled for gingerly dipping two fingers in and drawing them across our eyes and mouth. Having what Mam called 'a lick and a promise.'

Dad loved the land and accepted that nature had to have a rest. Instead of grumbling about the cold earth, he just started planning for the spring. He would plant seeds in little trays, as well as potato 'sets' and place them under the big bed in which we slept.

In the 1920s men on the dole had to go on Wednesdays and Fridays to 'sign on' at Barrow's Labour Exchange. Dad hated breaking off whatever job he was engaged with, getting changed into his one and only outfit, best white shirt and brown tie, riding breeches, checked jacket with cap to match set at a jaunty angle, and highly polished brown leggings and boots. Dad was a good-looking man who took a pride in himself. He had neat regular features, a straight nose and square chin and was ruddy in complexion with warm, twinkling brown eyes. He was always freshly shaved, apart from his small military moustache neatly spiked at each side with some special wax out of a small tube. We used to watch him getting ready and would giggle as he twirled the ends of his moustache, fine-tuning it with the wax. When he set off for the labour exchange, he looked more like a country squire than one of the unemployed. On Fridays he received his dole money and also his Army disability pension.

With the dole money, he brought back some basic groceries including sugar, tea, a few slices of bacon, Stork margarine, bread, jam, and from the farmers' stalls in Barrow market he bought potatoes, onions, carrots, and whatever else was available to be bought cheaply. We waited hungrily for his return and watched hopefully while he laid out the shopping for Mam to inspect. Then, with a twinkle in his eye, Dad would put his hand in his pocket and bring out two small paper bags. One bag would contain a few chocolates which he would hand to Mam. Slowly, tantalising, he would open the other one and solemnly start doling out a few sweets to each of us. This was our small treat for we never received pocket money.

Katie's finely turned-out father, William, took great pride in his appearance despite their humble lifestyle.

Needless to say, the food was used up before the next Friday. Sometimes if there were a few shillings left out of the dole money, Dad would give them to Mam. The next day, Saturday, she would walk the 2 miles to Barrow market and spend an hour rummaging among the second-hand clothes stalls for clothes for us, which were all we ever got, if we were lucky. But to us, food was more important than clothes. Sometimes we were so hungry we crept into a farmer's field with a knife, and stole a couple of turnips or swedes, which we would eat raw. We also spent a lot of our time around Mrs Crabtree's piggery, noticing that the big bin of smelly swill was always full. Their pigs were always well-fed, but we didn't like the look of the swill, and never wanted to eat it!

One day to our astonishment we saw a bakery van stop in the lane, then the driver take out a wooden tray filled with buns and cakes which he took along to the piggery and tipped into a wooden bin. Mouths watering, we waited until he had driven away, then, pretending to be Red Indians we crawled through the long grass to the side of the piggery. With one eye on the bungalow in case Johnny or his wife, Marie, were looking out, we sidled up to the wooden box. Our eyes popped out at the sight of meat and potato pies, iced buns, jam tarts, currant squares, jam roly-poly and other delicious cakes, the like of which hitherto we had only seen in bakery shops. No doubt these delicacies were destined to be tipped into the swill! We fell upon them like hungry dogs, filling our empty rumbling bellies until we could eat no more. There were still lots of these goodies in the box so we pushed as many as we could up our jerseys, then got down our hands and knees again and scuttled through the long grass to our home as fast as we could.

Mam could only stare open-mouthed as we tipped our spoils onto the small table. Will grinning with triumph said,

'We saw the bakery van tipping stuff into a box at the piggery. We were so hungry, Mam, we ate as much as we could, and brought as much as we could back for you. I hope you're not angry with us for stealing!'

Mam was angry, very angry indeed, but not with us. She stared at the food we had put on the table and fumed,

'I think it's an absolute scandal that good food like this should go to feed pigs, when there are so many families starving in this town.'

After that we kept a closer eye than ever on the piggery, and whenever that blue van arrived with its bounty we made sure we ate our fill.

Mam was quite right about hundreds of families in the town starving. During the 1920s, those who lived in the small terraced houses and the tenements of Hindpool and Barrow Island had no gardens where the husband could grow food as our father did for us, and the largest families in these areas were the most deprived. This was of some concern to Barrow Council who decided to fund a scheme to help those most in need, and agreed to supply 'free meals' to the two eldest children where the family numbered five or more children and where the father was unemployed.

Mam and Dad were delighted when they received a letter stating that their two eldest children would be included in this scheme. The venue where the meals were cooked would be 'The National Kitchen'. This large black-painted building, its name painted boldly in white on the side walls, was situated in Farm Street, Barrow Island, which served meals in its canteen for nearby shipyard workers, and also began to supply them to the local school. Where children had to travel to this place they would be supplied with free tram tickets from their teacher at school. We received them on a Friday morning, enough to last us the following week. This was a new routine for us. We left home at seven in the morning, caught the tram at the lane end at Ocean Road telling the driver where we had to alight, because we didn't know where the 'Coffee House' stop was.

This was all very exciting, a new adventure. As we alighted at our stop and the tram rattled away down Michaelson Road towards the Town Hall, I gazed up in awe at the twin towers of the Devonshire Buildings. Made of red sandstone, these tenement blocks appeared huge and forbidding. Then my eyes were drawn to a notice in one of the tower windows. 'GOD IS NOT MOCKED'. This convinced me, that God lived in the tower, and even years afterwards when I had grown up, especially during the war, my eyes always strayed to that notice. However, the delicious smell of freshly baked bread, drifting over from Osborne's bakery, brought me back to earth, reminding me how hungry I was. Will had crossed the road and was waiting impatiently for me at the corner of Island Road.

Further along this road was St John's School which we entered along with a ragged and unruly crowd of children. We took our place at the table, and wrapped our cold hands thankfully around steaming mugs of cocoa, and stared disapprovingly at the tenement dwellers who were giving the caretaker's wife a hard time. Mindful of God close by in the tower, I felt afraid, and silently begged him not to class us with those

Local children in early twentieth-century Barrow. *(Courtesy of Barrow Museum)*

of bad behaviour. I wondered too, when they lived so close, why they didn't know God was in the tower.

The caretaker's wife, Mrs Dobson, a pleasant-faced motherly lady, was kept very busy passing plates of bread and jam, refilling our mugs with cocoa out of a large enamel jug, and quietly scolding the wild ones. When there was no food or cocoa left the children departed leaving a messy table behind them. We thanked Mrs Dobson who asked us our names. When we told her she beamed with pleasure.

'Well fancy that! You have the same names as my two children William and Kathleen. Don't forget to come back for your dinner!'

There was a regular and reliable tram service in those days. Sometimes to our great pleasure the driver would be a friend of Dad's, Jim Flatman, whom we called 'Uncle Jim.' He seemed as glad to see us as we were of him for he always gave us a penny each. This enabled us to look forward to the luxury of the Saturday matinee at Walney Cinema, Charlie Chaplin films and Cowboys and Indians. And we loved those serials where the hero was left clinging to the edge of the cliff, or the heroine was tied to the railway line, and we had to wait until the following week to see what happened next!

We would leave school again at noon to catch the tram to Barrow Island and St John's School, eager for the 'free' dinner. This arrived in huge tins from the National Kitchen, steaming hot, with meaty aromas that wafted over us as the lids were removed and Mr Dobson helped Mrs Dobson dish the food out onto plates. The first time, the dinner was a very tasty hotpot with lots of crisply curling slices of potato on top of the meat and vegetables.

The tenement children behaved in a disorderly manner at the table, throwing bits of browned potato at each other instead of tucking in. When the food on our plates was eaten, Mrs Dobson offered us second helpings which we accepted gratefully, even though we knew there was rice pudding waiting in another big tin. Because we were well behaved and ate up our dinners without making a mess, Mrs Dobson gave Will and I the job of taking the big tins back to the National Kitchen in Farm Street, a few minutes' walk away. The dinner tin had crispy pieces of potato stuck to the sides which we scraped off and ate as we went along. We had enjoyed the dinner, but we were unable to resist eating the crispy morsels that remained. And later we were eager to tell Mam all about the lovely meal.

The dinners varied from day to day, but were well prepared and of good quality. Some days it was steak and kidney pie topped by a golden crust and served with creamy mashed potatoes. Then there would be mince and mash, meat and potato pie, or stew, and there was always a pudding to follow. Either sponge smothered in sticky syrup topped with custard, spotted dick and custard, or semolina pudding, or sometimes jam squares with custard. Mam was always pleased to hear what we had been given for the main meal of the day, but sorry that Les was unable to enjoy the meal also. The breakfast was always the same, cocoa and jam sandwiches. One of my favourite jams was rhubarb, though they changed the jam on the bread now and again to raspberry or blackberry. But we were always hungry at that time in the morning so it didn't matter and we tucked into the sandwiches with gusto.

On Saturdays breakfast was also available, but no dinners. We found we were the only children who turned up on Saturdays, so had the steaming cocoa jugs and piles of bread and jam all to ourselves. The tenement dwellers never bothered to come across to the school. Mrs Dobson said she couldn't understand why their parents didn't seem to appreciate there was free food on offer. Unfortunately for us, the 'free meals' scheme was discontinued the following year. We never knew whether it was because of the children who failed to appear for them, or whether it was because of new councillors who were concerned with the cost cutting of their budget. Sad to say we never went back to St John's School or saw Mrs Dobson again, and we really missed her warm motherly attention and all those appetising dinners.

Chapter Five

I BECOME AN AVID READER

From the very beginning of moving into the field, Dad had worked out in a sensible, practical, way, of how to afford the materials he needed for his plans. Therefore out of his £1 pension he opened a monthly account with a hardware store in town. This enabled him to buy nails, second-hand tongue-and-groove timber, bricks and mortar for the foundation of the kitchen range, paint, tarpaulin for weather-proofing, glass for the windows, tools for the garden, and seeds. All of the scheming and planning must have been heartbreakingly slow for Dad, in his determination to make a start on the kitchen that Mam needed so badly. There were lively arguments between them caused by the grinding poverty and hardship. Mam would try to get him to delay his monthly payment to the hardware shop and give her the money to buy shoes or some item of clothing for one of us. But Dad was adamant, unwilling to break what he considered was a gentleman's agreement. After all, the money came out of his pension. I think that Mam was always resentful she never got anything out of this pension, though what he was doing with the money was of benefit to all of us.

There was rarely any money left out of the dole for clothes or shoes for us, which had become a real problem for poor Mam when there were now three of us attending school, as well as a younger brother and baby sister at home. Before that we had thought nothing about running around barefoot. We only became aware of our poverty when we began mixing with children at school. Many were just as poorly dressed as we were, but there were a lot who were better-off, nicely dressed and who we considered 'posh'. These richer ones, needless to say, looked down on us and the other shabby children whose fathers were, like ours, out of work.

The village children were especially cruel. On our way home from school they would chase us along the lane, calling us 'Percy Pig' and 'Gypsy'. We were not gypsies, just homeless people with nowhere else to live. Some lads who were bigger and older were real bullies. We often ran through the gate crying. Dad was angry as he hated bullies, and decided my brothers needed his help.

'You have to learn to defend yourselves, and protect your sister.'

Laying down his spade he hurried them around to the back of the caravan and began to give them some advice. He had done a bit of sparring in his Army days so gave the boys the benefit of his experience. Whenever he had a bit of time to spare he would give the lads a few mock rounds until he was sure they had the confidence to stick up for themselves. Will was always being picked on by a big lad called Freddy, who mocked him, calling him a sissy because of his fair curly hair. But the next time he tried it on he got the shock of his life. For instead of running away Will squared up to him with his fists and punched him on his fat nose which bled profusely. It was Freddy's turn to run home crying. He never picked on my brothers Will and Les again.

But not all the better-off people on Walney looked down on us just because we were poor and lived in a caravan. Many of those in the Beach Crescent row of aloof houses, and some of those families in pleasant villas on Biggar Bank were very kind indeed. Many a parcel of good quality children's clothing was given to us by the wives. Their husbands had important office jobs in Vickers and their wives and children were always well-dressed. I think they admired my father's efforts in creating a beautiful productive garden to feed his children, and the way he was trying to improve his humble home. He was not at all like many of the unemployed who hung around street corners, defeated, not trying to help themselves, and unable to see a way out.

I had become acutely aware as I got older of my shabby clothes, and especially of my scuffed-up, ragged sandals. Sometimes, on the way home from school, I would walk alongside a smartly-dressed family, who lived in a lovely villa on Biggar Bank Road. Their mother would smile sweetly at me, apparently having no objection to my walking alongside her well-dressed children. As for me, I was in awe of their clothes, and was fascinated by their elegant shoes. They had several pairs, black, brown and really posh patent leather, worn to match in with whatever outfits they were wearing. I could scarcely take my eyes off them. Beautiful soft leather they were, with a handsome, shiny, buckle on the instep, which reminded me of a portrait hanging inside the school of the Cavaliers who wore buckled shoes. In my childish innocence I linked this portrait with these children who wore the same distinctive footwear.

One day walking along from school with them, this lady, 'Mrs C' I'll call her, asked me to go home with them. I was absolutely overwhelmed as I accompanied the family to their nice villa. They all went inside but I stayed politely on the step as I hadn't been invited into the house. A few minutes later she came to the door smiling, carrying a huge parcel which she gave to me.

'Give this to your mummy and I hope she finds the things useful.'

'Thank you very much, Mam, I will.'

I flew home like the wind and couldn't wait for Mam to open the parcel. I kept hoping there would be something for me in the parcel, but there never was anything. The clothes in the parcels were always for my younger brothers and sisters. Feeling like Cinderella I ran into the bedroom and wept.

From the very beginning in the infants, I loved everything about school and adored my teachers who were opening up the world for me. I quickly mastered the alphabet and picked up reading and writing with enthusiasm. I loved books and reading and was quick at learning. When I reached the junior school I was thrilled to find there was a lending library, and children were allowed to borrow books to read at home. I was in there every day sometimes taking out two books at a time. Read them? I devoured them! Books took me out of my narrow, deprived existence, into other people's lives which fascinated me, and I was deeply admiring of the authors' ability to do this, to create these other worlds, these other people's lives. It was because of reading and the love of words that I became so interested in my English lessons. This subject along with History and Geography became the ones I enjoyed the most and put all my energy into.

Long before that, the first book I had ever begun reading was one I had found on the tip. The tip at the lower end of Beach Crescent was a fascinating place for poor children on the way home from school. We would poke around in the gravel with a stick to see what we could find because we had seen the trucks tipping household rubbish there. Will found a wooden top and a ball, and I found this book, an adult novel, which was far too advanced reading for my age. Clutching it gleefully, I rushed home and hid it under my pillow, but Mam fished the book out when she made the bed. I was dismayed when I came in from school a day later and found her absorbed in the novel.

'Mam! That's MY book, which I found on the tip.'

'It's for adults and not fit reading for a seven-year-old girl!'

She refused to give the book back to me, though I think she continued to read the story herself.

Books, it seemed, were for ever going to get me into trouble with Mam. I would sneak in through the half-finished kitchen, library books under my coat, then hide under the high bed where we slept, and with a lit candle to see by, I became absorbed in my book. I was oblivious to my mother calling my name to do some little job or run some errand for her. When she finally found me in my hiding place she dragged me out, and furious with anger, threw my precious book on the fire. Screaming, I flung myself forward and rescued it before it had begun to singe, but burning my fingers. She snatched it back from me.

'All you think about is sticking your nose in a book, after being at school all day reading. Isn't that enough for you? Go and bring the washing in!'

'Please! Mam! Don't throw my book on the fire! It belongs to the library at school. They could send you to prison! Please! Mam! Don't throw my book on the fire! It belongs to the library.

She threw back her head and laughed.

'That's what reading is doing to you, filling your head with silly imaginings. Now go and get that washing in before the rain starts!'

A little bubble of rebellion rose in me that day and face hot with childish rage I stared at her defiantly and stood my ground. But before I could speak she raised the book threateningly and I grabbed the worn

Mary with
Glenis, Katie's
first daughter.

old clothes basket and fled outside to the long line of washing that was
flapping in the breeze. After that I was careful to hide my books under
the bed. But sometimes, unable to resist the lure of reading, I went home
the long way round, by the Biggar Bank Road, passing by Mrs C's villa
where I had gone to collect the parcel. I would make my way to one of
the shelters facing the Irish Sea and sit and read to my heart's content.
But I always got into trouble with Mam for reading and being late home.

There was always something to do. Water had to be carried from the stand-pipe at the top of the field. Dad did the job when we were small, but now we were getting bigger this became a dreaded task that me, Will and Les had to share. We all hated this rotten job, carrying buckets of water down that rough field. Though we filled the buckets at the tap, the water slopped and spilled down our clothes and feet, so that by the time we reached the caravan the buckets had very little in them, while our shoes squelched with water. We quarrelled among ourselves about our turns, none of us wanted to carry those buckets of water.

Dad, who had enough to do with the building work and the garden to see to, sympathised with us, and devised a way to make the job easier. He knocked together four pieces of wood like a picture frame, and showed us how to carry water. We had to stand inside the frame, which was placed over the filled buckets, grasp the bucket handles, lift them and start walking. Will, who was the eldest and the biggest, carried the water at first, much later I had a turn, and later on Les. The frame kept the buckets steady and away from our legs, and proved to be a simple yet effective solution for the carrying of drinking water. But we still quarrelled, and dodged out of the job, if we could.

Dad had solved the problem of providing water for bathing, washing clothes, and the garden during the dry spells in summer, by placing four barrels at the corners of the caravan to catch rain water. On Friday nights Dad would fill the boiler from one of the barrels. Mam would bring in the big tin bath and place it in front to the fire. When the water was hot Mam would fill the bath, half hot and half cold, and throw in the flannel. One by one, we would be scrubbed with Lifebuoy carbolic soap from the head down. Next came a jug of water on our heads, a big towel wrapped around us, and we would step out, and the next one would step in. Mam used to be on her knees for this Friday night ritual, and complained of how much her back hurt. While she would be drying us and brushing our hair, Dad would clear up the mess and empty the soapy water on the rose bushes and cabbages. Mam was always glad when the job was finished and we stood around the fire glowing and clean.

Dad had also dug a deep well in the corner by the hedge for watering the garden. He warned us to not to go anywhere near, in case we fell in.

The only time we disobeyed him was when we chased a big rat down the field pelting it with sticks and stones until reaching the well, the rat disappeared. We didn't stop to see if the rat survived, but raced away up the field looking for more rats, which we regarded as enemies. We hated going outside at night to use the 'dry' toilet, a small shed Dad had erected over a deep hole containing a drum which he had to empty periodically. He had enclosed it in wood with a proper seat which was quite comfortable. But we imagined rats were scuttling outside because they wanted to steal the hens' eggs, so, when sitting on the seat, we banged our heels hard against the wood casing, hoping the noise would scare them off.

Chapter Six

A VISIT TO MAUD'S

Slowly because of the lack of money, but steadily because that was the sort of man Dad was, Mam's much-longed for and dreamed-of kitchen became a reality. 'Skinny' Maud, the village woman, who with her regular visits followed its progress with interest and was really impressed by Dad's industry, became a more frequent visitor than ever. When at last there was a cheerful fire burning in the black-leaded range which Mam had polished so energetically, and the brown teapot was steaming gently on the hob, Maud sat chatting with Mam who was glowing with pride. We really hated coming in from school hungry to find her sitting there drinking tea, with one eye on the big pot of Irish stew, and showing no sign of leaving, for we knew Mam would not begin to dish up our dinners.

Maud would sit there determinedly, licking her lips, her nostrils twitching as she breathed in the appetising smell, and swallowing hungrily, her Adam's apple bobbing up and down with longing. For all we knew, or cared, she may have been hungrier than we were, but we wanted our food.

'Isn't dinner ready yet, Mam? I'm hungry!' Will complained.

'So are we!' Les and I would chorus, forcing Mam to act. With Maud still sitting there as unmoveable as a sphinx, she would start ladling it out, and to our chagrin, included Maud, which meant less for us. She told us afterwards that it was manners to include her, but we could tell that she was cross that Maud herself had not had the manners to leave when she could see hungry children waiting for their meal. Mopping up his plate with a thick slice of bread, eight-year-old Will grumbled.

'She never invites us to her place, and gives us food!'

Mam grinned wryly, and looking around at her brood, pursed her lips.

'Well! You could hardly expect her to feed you lot, Will!'

But surprisingly, Maud did invite Mam to her little cobbled house in the village, and of course we children went too, one Saturday. We sat around her cramped living room, while she, stiff-backed and skinny, sat at a small organ playing the tunes of the day, as her way of entertaining us. Perhaps she thought we needed some culture! Will, bored stiff and longing to go home as we all were, sat watching Maud's ginger cat sleeping in the oven of the old range. Then out of boredom and pure mischief he slyly shut the oven door, and sat waiting to see what would happen. A little later, a terrible high-pitched mewling, and scratching on the oven door brought Maud's musical concert to an end, and she flew to the oven and opened the door. Wild-eyed, the cat shot out, a ginger streak of feline fury, and began capering about all over the room, sending Will into hysterical shrieks of laughter. Maud screeched, 'You wicked, wicked boy!' and turning to Mam, said curtly, 'I think you had all better go!'

No doubt Will thought that would bring an end to Maud's visits to our place, but she appeared the next week as though nothing had happened. And as usual if there were pots simmering on the stove, she would sit there solidly, until Mam was forced to start dishing out our dinners. The 'Maud the merrier' it was not. Will resented her sitting at our table eating our food. Sometimes Dad would come in for a cup of tea, but if he saw Maud there, he would help himself to a cup of water out of the bucket that stood in the scullery, and scurry back to the haven of his garden.

Maud was never there of an evening, which we were glad about. We loved to sit on the rag-rug facing the fire and listen to Mam talking about her childhood in Galway, or reciting little poems to us. A favourite of mine was about the mouse and the cake which was meant to teach us not to be greedy. It went like this:

A mouse found a piece of the richest plum cake.
'Here's a treasure', said he. 'What a feast it will make.

Ah! What is that noise? 'Tis my brothers at play.
I must hide with the cake, lest they wander this way.'
He gobbled it up without leaving a mess.
But was soon so unwell, he groaned in distress.
The mouse doctor came and said 'Ah! It's too late,
you must die before long so prepare for your fate.
If only you'd shared that cake with your brothers,
it would have done you no harm, and would have been good for the others.'
So now little children a lesson may take,
don't be selfish and greedy like the mouse and the cake.

Will, who always had a sense of adventure enjoyed the one which went:

Three little people
sat down to chat,
a very long time ago,
they all of them thought the earth was flat,
for somebody told them so . . .

The rest of the poem eludes me, but was on the theme of setting out to discover if it was true. Will liked it, so probably remembered it better than I have. Mam enjoyed these cosy evenings in front of the new range as much as we did. She often said they were the happiest days of her life.

As well as completing the kitchen, and scullery, Dad had included an outhouse for a wash boiler, which also contained a bench where he could repair shoes. Before that the boiler had stood outside in the open, so now Mam was under shelter on wash days, which made life easier for her. Our three-year-old brother, Ronnie, whom we were to lose that year, 1928, delighted in gathering little sticks for her which he put in a neat pile next to the boiler. It was his way of helping, which Mam thought about often. She spoke about her 'little helper' for years afterwards and never ever got over losing him. Some of her previous joy of living and fun went out of her and she was never quite the same woman again.

Home was a more comfortable place now for all of us. By frequent visits to the town's salerooms with his flat handcart, Dad had bought

Katie and her brother Will with Snowball in about 1923.

a table, chairs, a sideboard, a horsehair sofa and two old armchairs. He had also covered the wooden floor with cheerful red linoleum, in an effort to link the kitchen floor with the red lino in the van. There was space to sit at the table doing homework, and for reading. For lighting there were two sturdy paraffin oil lamps with glass shades. In the caravan we only had candles. The original caravan now became 'the parlour' as well as the bedrooms. Dad partitioned off some of the huge area of the kitchen to form two small bedrooms for the future. Because we were a mixed family which was growing older, it was necessary, and decent, that in future I would have my own room and bed.

Outside the garden continued to flourish, and our white goat, which was named Snowball, munched contentedly in the corner of the field.

The first year in the field when Dad bought her, he was so pleased he got the owner to take a photo of me and Will standing each side of the goat. On such a bitterly cold day we both shivered and started to cry. Mam soothed us and promised we would enjoy the goat's milk after it had given birth to a kid. However, this never happened for Snowball failed to become pregnant. In the end she became the family pet until Dad decided to extend his garden, and had to sell her.

At the back of the 'house' Dad gradually added a few more pullets and a fierce-eyed, red-feathered cockerel to live in the hen-hut, and who'd scratch around in the wire-enclosed run for insects. He was delighted if a hen became broody and sat on eggs, so kept a close eye on them until they were due to be hatched. Then he would bring the eggs in and place them on an old blanket in the warmth of the oven. Mam would check on them and as soon as cracks appeared on the shells she would bring them out of the oven and lay them on a sheet of newspaper on the kitchen floor. We would gather round fascinated as the little chicks inside the shells pecked their way out of their prison and stood on stick-like legs with bits of shell sticking to their wet bodies. This soon dried and fell off, leaving them a soft fluffy yellow, chirping sharply, and with black eyes bright and alert. Having no toys, or pets now that Snowball had gone, we adored them, and loved to watch them eating the hard-boiled egg which Mam had chopped up for them.

Dad had also bought a drake and a few ducks, one of which became broody. Dad noticed her waddling off to the shelter of the hedge, and when he went to investigate, found her sitting contentedly on a clutch of green eggs. Some time later, she emerged proudly from her nest under the hedge with five fluffy ducklings waddling behind. We loved them even more than the yellow chicks as they seemed to stay fluffy much longer. Once the chicks lost their fluff their new adult feathers made them look scrawny and less attractive.

Life seemed at last to be running the way Dad had envisaged. The garden was flourishing and the hens were laying regularly as the weather warmed up, so we were able to have fresh eggs as well as fresh vegetables. One of our favourite meals in early summer was a dinner of lovely new potatoes, fresh green cabbage and a newly-laid, fried

Katie's sister Evelyn with Mary in Barrow in the 1940s.

egg. We would enjoy breaking the yolk so that we could dip pieces of potato in its golden freshness. Sunday morning breakfast, too, was looked forward to. Moving about quietly so as not to wake our baby sister Evelyn, Mam would start preparing the breakfast. Instead of the usual porridge, Mam would cook tasty bacon with fried bread, heat up tinned tomatoes, and Dad would come in from the garden, wash his hands, and help her to dish up. Happy Sunday morning breakfasts they were, and now that Mam had the cooking range we had lovely dinners too.

Sometimes if Dad had given her a few shillings left from the dole, she would hurry to Barrow market on the Saturday. There she would buy shin beef and a half of a cow heel, and on Sundays she would chop the beef and cow heel, add onions and carrots out of Dad's garden, and put them in a big brown stew pot with a little water, salt and pepper and put them in the oven to cook slowly, with a rice pudding on the shelf below. While the stew was cooking there was the most delicious aroma in the kitchen, and when all was ready, Mam would dish up the dinner. We had lovely mashed potatoes and cauliflower or cabbage with the stew, which was oozing with rich gravy. A dinner 'fit for a king' Dad used to say. To follow it we would have the creamy rice pudding covered by an enticing brown skin on top. When the stew was used up, Mam would give us the little bones from the cow heel which were smooth and ideal for playing a little game, tossing them over and over our hands, a bit like juggling.

On other Sundays Mam would roast a bit of brisket, a cheap cut of beef done slowly in the oven with vegetables and potatoes roasted to go with it. As it was a fatty cut of beef there'd be some rich dripping left which Mam saved in a jam-jar and which was delicious on bread. What was left on the bone would be put in the big iron pot with onions, carrots and potatoes to cook on the top of the stove as a stew for Monday's dinner.

These were our 'good times', mainly in the summer when there were lots of young vegetables in the garden. And in the evenings Dad would sit in one of the old armchairs and play on his piano-accordion all the old songs from the First World War, and some Irish ones that Mam loved as she came from Galway. Both doors would be open to let in a gentle breeze. A lovely perfume from the sweet-peas and the climbing roses on the trellis would waft straight in through the open door at the front which was the caravan, but now became the 'parlour' as well as the bedroom. We had no radio so enjoyed Dad's playing very much. Later on Dad got an old wind-up gramophone with a huge horn from the sale-room. There was only one record so we replayed this recording over and over; driving Mam crazy until she got us a few more records from a market stall.

Our lives were happy, though we were poor and only had simple pleasures, such as going up the field to Biggar Bank. This 'Bank' facing the Irish Sea was our playground where there were swings, a seesaw, and a wooden roundabout.

Les had made friends with a boy of his age, called Frank, whose parents managed the West Shore Bowling Club on Biggar Bank. We loved watching through a gap in the hedge, if a game of bowls was in progress, fascinated by the sight of shiny black balls rolling smoothly on the velvety square of green grass, so superbly kept by Frank's father. This game must have been a male preserve in those days, for I never ever saw any ladies taking part.

If Frank was allowed out to play he used to come with us to where we would be joined by other lads from Beach Crescent, for a game of cricket. I used to enjoy this activity, but was peeved by always being a fielder. I was never allowed near the wicket, either to bat, or to bowl. Lads used to assume that a girl could not bowl a ball, or handle a bat. In fact I was only tolerated because of my two brothers, Will and Les. Cricket also seemed to be a male preserve. Because I was always with my brothers, I suppose everyone considered me to be a 'tomboy'. I only knew two girls who lived on Biggar Bank; sometimes I would join them on the swings, but I was mostly with the lads who played with my brothers.

When the tide was out we loved to go winkling with an old pan. We would take our shoes off and paddle in the small pools between the rocks. Small crabs would scuttle over our bare feet when we turned over the rocks looking for winkles. We would have to keep a sharp lookout for when the tide turned as the water would come in quite suddenly in two long arms, which was very dangerous and surprisingly fast, encircling anyone who had failed to keep watch. Dad had warned us about this many times, so we always remembered to keep watching for the tide to turn.

Once we found some tins of fruit among the seaweed, and greatly excited we rushed home with our bounty. Mam made a pan of creamy custard to pour over the peaches, a rare treat for us. But to our intense disappointment, when Mam opened the tins they were so pickled with salt, it was impossible to eat them. Seeing how upset we were she went outside to Dad and asked him to pull up a few sticks of rhubarb, to have with the custard. Dad said the tins must have been in the sea a very long time to have become so infected with salt.

There was a lot of fun in eagerly walking along the lines of seaweed, beach-combing, to see what we could find. Often, Dad would come as well looking for pieces of timber that would come in useful for his building projects. Sometimes after Vickers had launched a new ocean liner, pieces of timber used to shore-up the launching pad, would be flung off into the channel as the stern end of the vessel hit the water. These planks of wood were carried away by the tides and then, when the tide turned, swept into the shore at Biggar Bank.

In good weather of a weekend, Biggar Bank was crowded with people from the town, especially during Easter, the Bank Holidays of Whitsuntide, of August and in the summer. At these times travelling fairs visited, bringing colour, gaiety, and vibrant life to the long stretch of grassy emptiness that was Walney Island's shore. The gaudily painted caravans which somehow we didn't associate with our own 'home', the novelty stalls, coconut shies, swing boats, side shows, and best of all, the merry-go-round with its constant music blaring out that added to the excitement. How we loved these fairs!

We would stand rooted to the spot staring at the brightly coloured hobby-horses and other animals and the lucky children who sat astride them as they went round and around for a penny. We had no money to participate, but we were fascinated and envious watching others enjoying these magical rides. In the centre of the merry-go-round

The pavilion at Biggar Bank in about 1905.

there was a colourful organ with imitation musicians, small figures beating time. And there was the constant throbbing from the steam locomotive close by that gave the merry-go-round its power. We loved being among the crowds of parents standing around watching, while their children waited for a turn, some of them eating candy floss or licking ice-cream.

We also enjoyed watching people at the coconut stall energetically throwing wooden balls trying to knock a coconut down. The stall owner would be shouting constantly, 'Three balls a penny! Five down to win!' Will and Les itched to have a go so that they could win a coconut to take home. Mam would never come with us because she knew we would pester her like crazy for money which she did not have. She must have been glad when the fair packed up and left, but we were sorry and hoped the next time they came we'd have a couple of pennies. Like all children we were impatient for the good times, such as playing on Biggar Bank, Christmas, the early summer, school holidays, longer and sunnier days and those enjoyable Sundays of better meals and Dad playing the accordion. This was one of the days we always looked forward to, which we thought would be the same for ever, until that terrible Sunday in June 1928.

Chapter Seven

FAMILY LOSS

I was about seven-and-a-half years old at the time, but I have never forgotten that day or the many horrific ones that followed. It was a warm, sunny June morning, the air balmy but clean and fresh, with the promise of a lovely summer on the horizon. It was a happy family scene, the bare scrubbed table simply laid, Dad busy dishing out bacon, fried bread and hot tomatoes on the warmed plates, Mam at the stove reaching for the big brown teapot. The four of us, Will, Les, me, and three-year-old Ronnie, were all sat obediently on the old horsehair couch, eyes turned expectantly towards Dad, waiting for him to say, 'You can come to the table now.' If we made any move towards the table too early we would earn a stern rebuke from Dad who was a stickler for manners and politeness.

I do not know to this day, writing my memories of this tragic event, why, or how it should have happened, but as Mam turned from the range with the brown teapot in her hand, little Ronnie left my side on the couch, and ran smack bang into her. The teapot smashed to pieces, sending the hot scalding liquid and tea-leaves cascading all over his head and shoulders. Poor Mam, crying, frantic and horror-stricken was struggling trying to get the hot wet clothes over the screaming child's head, while Dad rushed across to the mantelpiece for the big scissors and began to cut the clothes away. From the couch, shocked and terrified, I have never ever forgotten this. Or the running down the lane and along Ocean Road to Vickerstown with a note clutched in my hand for Mrs Crabtree, and running back home again grasping bandages and a bottle of some special oil which she was sending for Mam to apply to poor little Ronnie's scalded body.

I don't know if anyone ate the special breakfast that morning – we were all too stunned by what had happened. But nature protects the minds of young children by drawing a veil over harrowing events, thus enabling the children to resume their innocent play and normal routines. But these events remain stored in the subconscious from where they emerge in later life as this did with me many times.

For our parents the horror and shock of what had happened sat heavily on their shoulders. With them the grim awareness of the accident was ever-present. The sight of a beloved child swathed in bandages and only half-conscious must have been very hard for them to bear. I sat nursing him after I came in from school on the Monday to enable Mam to make the dinner. He was murmuring 'Katty, I'm falling.' And I said, 'No, you're not, Ronnie! I'm holding you tight.'

He must have worsened, for on the Tuesday when we were in school Mam wheeled him into town to the hospital in a little trolley, and we returned from school to find our parents silent and pale-faced, going about their routine without speaking. A black cloud seemed to have settled on the household and refused to go away.

The next day, Wednesday, I had only been in class about two hours when my Dad was ushered in by the head teacher. I had no idea why he was there as he stood talking in low tones to my teacher. She was nodding slowly her face serious and understanding. Looking across at me she raised her hand and beckoned me forward. The class was full of curiosity and whispering together behind their hands as I followed my father out of the class and went to the cloakroom for my coat. On the way home I asked, 'What's wrong, Dad? Why are you taking me home?'

His usually ruddy face pale, he was silent for a few minutes as though he was trying to find the right words. Then he said quietly, 'We have to go to the hospital. Ronnie has taken a turn for the worse. Mam wants you to mind the baby while we are away.'

Even though I was only seven-and-a-half, I was well used to looking after my younger siblings. In fact it was always me who ran for the midwife. Minding the baby was one of the 'jobs' that awaited me when I got home from school. I had always watched my mother the way she did things, and was quite adept at changing nappies, giving babies their bottle, and rocking them to sleep. My sister, Evelyn, was a placid baby and quite easy to mind, and while she slept I was often able to read a few pages out of my library book. Mam had made a pile of sandwiches of bread and jam to 'put us on' until she returned to give us our dinner. They seemed to be gone for hours. Will and Les arrived home from school and the sandwiches soon disappeared. However, Mam had cooked some new potatoes and cabbage and left them to one side. Because we were hungry by six o'clock and they had not returned we ate them cold.

We never learned what had happened until the next day. We returned from school to find the curtains drawn and our parents sitting together on the old couch, submerged in grief. Mam said brokenly, 'Ronnie has died and gone to heaven.' We all sat down and cried with them.

There was much coming and going the next few days. People called in to comfort Mam, shocked at the news, and anxious to help, for poor people like us had no money for funerals. Granny Thornton, a lovely lady from Ocean Road who had been kind to Mam and Dad, was there every day. And Skinny Maud, in spite of how she appeared to us children, proved to be a very staunch friend of our family. With Granny Thornton she tramped all over Walney, knocking at doors, appealing for help for our stricken family, collecting money from those who could afford it. Dad went into town to engage an undertaker while Mam moved around the home, white-faced and grieving for the loss of a beloved child, and no doubt asking herself over and over again why it had to happen. Her luxurious hair looked dull and lifeless strained back into an unattractive bun on her white neck.

Then, on another terrible day we returned from school to find a long shiny box in the parlour set up on two trestles. Beside it rested the lid, with Ronnie's name and date on it. A lit candle cast eerie shadows around the wall. I was terrified having to pass by on my way to bed; that marble statue in the box surrounded by lace couldn't be my adorable little brother of the angelic features big blue eyes and flaxen hair. In the three days the box was there, I often found Mam sitting there weeping. There was a strange scent from the spray of arum lilies someone had brought and the smell of new varnish which somehow added to the

Maritime Museum Walk in 2007 with Jubilee Bridge and Walney in the background.

horror of what had happened. Ever since I have always associated those scents with death, and felt very afraid.

On the day of the funeral Mam kept us off school. People were coming in and bringing things. Granny Thornton lent Mam a lovely lace tablecloth, cutlery, some nice china and glass dishes, and some of the other women brought ham sandwiches, a tin of creamy milk, and opened tins of pineapple chunks which they emptied into a large glass dish. We were bemused, we never had parties, and didn't know why there should be one that day. Children were kept in the dark about most things in those days.

Outside in the lane the glass hearse arrived, drawn along by shiny black horses with their manes decorated with ebony-black plumes. They stood in their shafts waiting patiently. Men in deep black with tall shiny top-hats entered our home and prepared to put the lid on the shiny box. One by one Mam lifted us up to kiss our little brother goodbye but I stiffened and screamed as my lips touched that cold marble face. Then my Mam laid a crucifix in his little hands, the men in black moved forward, put on the lid and screwed it down. Solemnly, they carried him away from his home and down the garden path to the waiting hearse. Mam and Dad with the visitors behind them formed a small line behind the hearse waiting for it to move. We three stood on the path watching, and listening to the rhythmic clip-clop of the horses' hooves as the sad procession moved slowly down the lane and out of our sight on their way to St Mary's Church and the cemetery near the Promenade. The events we witnessed seemed so unreal, like scenes at the cinema.

Running back into the darkened kitchen we gathered around the table staring at the food with mouths watering. The light from one oil-lamp which was turned down low, flickered on the borrowed china and cutlery, but it was on the big glass dish of pineapple chunks glistening invitingly that our eyes focussed. Mam had warned us not to touch anything. We looked at the shining fruit piled up, then at each other, and back again to the fruit, our mouths watering. Will whispered, 'We could have one each . . . they wouldn't miss three lumps.'

We stared at each other remembering what Mam had said and hesitated. Then making the decision for us all, Will picked up a spoon and ladled three chunks out one at a time and gave us one each. We had never tasted such a juicy exotic piece of fruit before, and savoured it slowly before swallowing it with a sigh of pleasure but eager for more, and hoping the visitors wouldn't eat them all. Afterwards we eyed the dish longingly, though I was wondering if anyone would notice that three chunks were missing, but felt sure the women hadn't counted them. Then resolutely, we turned our backs on the table remembering our promise. We each had been given jobs to do, Will and Les had to bring fresh water from the tap, I had to keep the place tidy, and give baby Evelyn her bottle when she woke up. Maybe my brothers soon forgot about 'stealing' the three pineapple chunks on the day of our little brother's funeral, but I remembered, and felt guilty about it for a long time.

I noticed there was a coldness developing between Mam and Dad since the terrible events of early June. They seemed to be arguing a lot more. One afternoon when coming home from school, I was horrified when I heard harsh words being spoken between them. When the accident had happened they had each tried to comfort the other. But now they were actually blaming each other for what had happened. Mam, in a shrill

Mary in Barrow.

harsh voice, was accusing Dad of being too strict with us. That he had shouted at Ronnie causing him to run towards her.

Dad retaliated very angrily and shouted,

'Don't try to blame me! I told you many times to get rid of that bloody cracked teapot that you kept stewing on the stove. They are cheap enough in the market!'

'Cheap? Why didn't you buy one then? You hang on to all the money! I don't get the chance to buy anything.'

Mam's voice was shrill and very bitter. I did not want to wait to hear the rest of the argument. Hugging my library books I fled up the field sobbing. There had often been arguments, mostly about the lack of money, but they had always ended amicably. There had been none of this searing bitterness which had been brought about by the tragedy that had befallen our family and changed Mam irrevocably. The healing was to take a long time to begin.

I came home from school one afternoon in early July to find Dad carefully picking some flowers out of the wonderful summer display that bordered the crazy-paved path. He stood up, and said to me, 'I'm taking these flowers to Ronnie's grave. Your Mam won't come with me – she said it's too soon. Perhaps you'd like to come?'

I hesitated uneasily, not really wanting to go to this strange place. 'Can I see if it's alright with Mam first?'

He nodded and went back to selecting some more blooms while I ran into the kitchen where Mam was busy at the range. When I asked her if it was alright for me to go with Dad, her voice was muffled as she answered without turning, 'Yes, if you want to. I'm too tired.'

Dad had picked a small bunch of climbing roses and sweet-peas from off the trellis and gave them to me. We took about thirty minutes to walk to St Mary's cemetery near the Promenade. St Mary's Church and graveyard was on a hill that overlooked the channel and Vickers Shipyard. After we had passed through the big gates and climbed the path I felt very frightened by the sight of all those tombstones, and wished I had not gone to see Ronnie in his grave. I had imagined a hole with a shiny box in it, but instead there was this mound of earth with bunches of withered flowers covering it. Dad, forever the gardener, began tidying away all the dead flowers and taking them to a rubbish box with me following, afraid to be alone among all those tilting headstones. There was a water tap there so he filled a big jam-jar he'd brought for water and we returned to the graveside, where Dad gathered up his lovely summer flowers and together with my posy put them in the jar and placed it on the mound. For ever after that I associated churches with death and gravestones and never wanted to go near such a place again.

Chapter Eight

HOSPITAL

E ach year health visitors came to the school to examine our heads to see if we had lice in our hair. If we were 'guilty', we would be given a note to take home which made us feel ashamed – an outcast. The remedy was the use of a fine toothcomb and the anointment of our head with some horrid-smelling oil called sassafras which made us stink like a skunk and we had to stay off school until our hair was washed clean again.

Doctors came too, to test our eyesight, our breathing, and look into our throats. I think I was about nine years old when I had my throat looked into and had to take a note home for our parents. Les had one also, and so it seemed had a lot of other children. In the 1920s if a child was found to have swollen tonsils, the doctors' rule seemed to be 'whip them out!' I heard Mam talking to some mothers who lived farther up the field from us about it. I heard one of them say, 'it's going to be a big day at the hospital!'

In my innocence I imagined it to be something to do with the Hospital Carnival – Mam had taken us all once to see it pass by the Town Hall. I remembered my excitement at watching the wonderfully decorated floats and flower-bedecked carts, especially the one where the Carnival Queen sat there in all her finery surrounded by a retinue of pretty girls. Is that what Les and I were going to be part of? I could hardly wait. It had never been explained to us that we were to have operations.

When the 'Big Day' finally arrived, we travelled on the tram from Walney to the hospital in Barrow. To my astonishment the waiting room was crowded with kids and their mothers. Our Mam looked white-faced and haunted. I didn't know why she looked so overwrought, but I learned later, this was the same hospital where my little brother had died two years earlier. Nurses came in and fitted us out with white gowns, hats and long white socks and the kids whooped with glee. It was great fun, almost a pantomime, as one by one the kids disappeared into the corridor with a nurse. We all craned our necks each time the door opened in an effort to see into this mysterious place where the kids were getting ready for the carnival. I was green with envy when my brother Les was swept in ahead of me.

When my turn came I literally danced down the corridor and into this 'theatre'. Once inside I came to an abrupt halt and stared around in horror. The floor was spattered with blood and discarded bits of flesh: tonsils. My mouth opened in a shrill scream of terror as eager hands reached out. I turned to flee for my life, but four pairs of strong arms fastened on me and I was swung aloft on to a table. A huge lamp like the angry eye of God swayed crazily overhead as I struggled like a wild thing. Then someone pushed a mask on my face, as if trying to kill me.

Some lost time later I opened my eyes, relieved to find I was still alive after all. But my head throbbed like a fairground engine, my throat felt like I had been on the block in the Tower of London, and all around me was the heavy and sickly smell of chloroform. There were bodies strewn around the floor huddled in blankets, but as I got my eyes into focus I was comforted to see Les was beginning to move around. As that happened, the nurses beckoned our mother. We were then stood unceremoniously on our feet and bundled into our hats and coats. All round us, kids were bewildered and crying, and some were being sick. Pale and exhausted from the ordeal of waiting, Mam was struggling to get us through the doorway when a lady who knew Mam offered us a lift to the Promenade. She had a taxi waiting to take her and her little girl to their home in North Scale village. Our Mam thanked her and we clambered groggily into its comforting interior.

Ten minutes later, we left the warmth of the taxi, and stood at the Promenade tram stop. There was a cold wind coming from the channel, and poor Les was as white as a sheet as we stood there shivering and waiting for the tram. Suddenly I was sick, vomiting blood. I stared terrified, as the red pool spread all over the pavement. Poor Mam, close

Mary with Cary, Katie's second daughter, in 1953.

to tears, somehow managed to get us on the tram which dropped us at the junction of Ocean Road and Carr Lane. Then she had to struggle up the lane, hampered by the weight of two drooping children who were suffering from the effects of the ether. We had scarcely enough energy to put one foot in front of the other. I remember vividly how leaden my feet and legs felt.

Dad must have looked up from his garden, saw our agonisingly slow progress, and came to meet us pushing his handcart. Mam greatly relieved, smiled more warmly towards him than she had done for a long time. Scooping us up in his arms and laying us onto the handcart, he said, winking at Mam, said, 'Gosh Mary! What are you feeding them on?'

This remark made me giggle, and moan thickly that my throat hurt, while poor Les just managed a sickly smile. The floor of the cart was hard, but I was relieved to be able to lie down, instead of struggling to walk. Mam, smiling her gratitude for him arriving so promptly, helped him to push the handcart along the lane. We were both very hungry when we reached home but found that even swallowing a mouthful of water was agonising, never mind food. Mam made us some thin sweet custard which we slowly and painfully, drank from cups. And for the next few days we drank thin gruel porridge, and some more thin custard, and we were kept off school for the rest of that week. We both envied Will coming in from school and tucking in to the usual dinners and hunks of bread and dripping, and wondered why he hadn't had this awful operation. But by the following week we, too, were back at school and recovering the ability to swallow without pain, which was a great relief to Mam.

The black cloud that had descended on our family two years earlier, seemed to be lifting, and Mam was becoming plump and contented-looking again. Her auburn hair had recovered some of its lustre and was tumbling in luxurious waves down her back once more, and she looked happier. Later on that year, November 1930, brought her the gift of another child, a boy. Once again I had to run to Vickerstown with a note for a nurse, a midwife she was called, I learned later. This had always been one of my jobs because I was the eldest girl in the family. As I returned home the nurse passed me, riding her old sit-up-and-beg bicycle with the big bag strapped behind the saddle.

I had always presumed that the new baby came in that bag, for I was never told why Mam was laid up in bed as though she was ill. Mam was a very fit woman and never ever ailed. Ronnie's accident and death had been a terrible shock to her, and she was never quite the same again. She still grieved. I often saw tears running down her cheeks as she bathed this new baby boy, though he seemed to have healed a lot of the pain for her. Perhaps she thought this boy was in place of the one she had lost, I do not know, but nevertheless, she gave him the same name, Ronald. Of course this was another mouth to feed, but Mam was a great believer in breastfeeding and didn't seem to need any extra food to enable her to keep this up for months. But Dad always brought her a few bottles of Guinness which she enjoyed and which she believed helped her to produce milk for the baby.

Chapter Nine

CLOGS

Each day after school, Les and I had to take a jug and go to the big house on Tummer Hill to buy the household milk. The house was situated near Ocean Road where a hard-working couple with three children lived. Mrs B took in house guests who came from as far afield as Manchester. They also had a farm in Biggar Village, and the husband sold milk around the doors on Walney. When Mrs B came to the door in answer to our knock, we would chorus, 'a pint of milk, please!' She would take our jug across to the dairy and ladle out the milk which always seemed to us a very generous measure. When we handed her the pennies in payment, she always asked us to wait. When she returned she handed us a big slice of apple pie or cake to eat on the way home. We never left her house without something nice to eat. She was, without doubt, a very generous, kind-hearted lady.

One very memorable day when Les and I had gone after school to buy the milk, Mrs B gave us a piece of apple pie and asked us to wait. I put the jug down on the step so that I could sample the delights of her apple pie. By the time we had both eaten our thick slice of pie, she returned and handed me a large brown parcel which I thanked her for. Les picked up our milk jug from the step and both very excited and wondering what was in the parcel, we set off slowly along the lane with Les casting anxious blue eyes on the milk slopping about in the jug. I had always carried it before, so he didn't want to spill any.

Later, when we arrived home Mam's eyes shone, as she began opening the parcel. She lifted out pretty dresses and good quality coats that fitted my younger sister, Evelyn, and shirts and pants and neatly darned socks suitable for Les, but nothing for Will or me as we were older. I watched

Evelyn and Mary enjoying Walney Beach in the 1950s.

with sinking heart as my Mam tried these lovely things on the younger children. It was then I spotted the boots. Quick as a silver-fish I thrust my feet into them, admiring their well-polished uppers, just as Mam turned around. She frowned, eyeing them doubtfully.

'They look too small for you!'

Stubbornly, I kept insisting they fitted me well. I had pushed my old broken sandals under the couch out of sight. I was determined not to stay away from school.

But oh! How I suffered the following day. The girls in my class all tittered at me for wearing boys' boots and chased me all over the playground, separating me from friend, Jenny, and calling us both nasty names. One spiteful girl deliberately stamped on my toes just to get a laugh from her cronies. The boots were too small for me, and I felt crippled by their tightness. Unusually for me, I was glad when home-time came. To avoid the other girls I hid in the toilet until they had all gone. Slowly and painfully I then began to make my way home wishing I had never taken the boots.

The lane that day seemed to be twice as long as normal. In the distance I could make out a pale blob between the small curtains of the kitchen window, Mam was watching and waiting. Tears sprang to my eyes but I dashed them angrily away and howled into the wind.

'Mam doesn't care about my pain, so long as I'm home to do another job, or mind the baby!'

I flung myself down on the rough grass near the lane in a dejected heap, the misery of the day crowding out the pleasure of two new library books which lay beside me. In my mind I could still hear the laughter and jeering at the boots, the name-calling – 'Gypsy, gypsy in little boys' boots!' And remember too, all the sneering that had gone on about my best friend, Jenny. They would shout, 'Stinky Jenny Maddock! She smells of Finny Haddock!' Just because sometimes Jenny worked in a wet-fish shop on a Saturday! Now, I had Mam to face. I could see she was still watching, but jerked my face away from that window and stared unhappily through swimming blue eyes across the marsh.

A black-headed gull which had been hovering above me in the hope that I may give him some tit-bits gave up and soared away. I watched his flight across the salt marsh until he was just a speck over the shipyard cranes. From there came the constant hammering which went on day and night on the construction of the new liner cradled in the docks. Longing to remove the boots from my poor feet, I stared at the distant channel wishing the tide was in so that I could have a paddle in the salt water to ease them, and sighed heavily. Finally, picking up my books, I stumbled along the lane, grimacing with every step, on my way home to face Mam's anger.

As soon as I entered the door she met me, with a face like thunder. 'Take those blasted boots off!'

She hustled me into the kitchen. 'I told you yesterday they were too small!' she said as she wrenched them none-too-gently off my feet.

'Crippling yourself you are – you silly girl!' She gave me a sharp slap on the leg. 'And what a mess you've made them!' She picked up a corner of her sack apron and gave them a brisk rub.

Miserably, I curled up in the old armchair and began rubbing my sore feet. They were as cold as ice from being cramped in the boots. My toes bore angry red patches where the leather had pressed against the skin and from being stamped on. Resentful and unhappy I watched her trying the boots on Les's feet. They fitted him easily as Mam had known they would.

'Now you can go back to school, son, and she can take a turn at staying home!'

'No! No! I don't want to stay off school! It's not fair! I never get anything given to me!'

I turned my face into the chair and wept, not for the boots, but because I hated missing school. Mam knew this and relenting a little, gave my shoulder a small, sympathetic squeeze.

'They are BOYS' boots, anyway!'

Later I heard her berating Dad fiercely about this situation. 'Why do you never notice when the kids need things? Why can't you put a few shillings to one side for them? If you looked up from the garden now and again, you would see both Will and Katie need shoes. I never see a decent second-hand pair on the market stalls.'

The following Friday when Dad went to sign on and collect his dole and Army pension, he not only arrived home with the usual grocery shopping, he carried two brown paper bags as well. Out of one bag came a pair of black laced-up clogs for Will. Beaming, with pleasure, eleven-year-old Will tried them on and pranced about the kitchen testing them.

'Those village lads had better not start on me again! Not now I have these on my feet!' said Will.

Dad frowned and warned him severely. 'Will! They are not weapons to fight with! Use your fists like I showed you if anyone starts bullying you!'

From the other bag Dad brought out a pair of 'fancy' red clogs that fastened across the ankles with a strap and buttons, and gave them to me to try on. They fitted me comfortably and Dad assured us that our feet would be warm and dry. I stared down at my new red clogs doubtfully. 'Silly me,' I thought biting my lip, 'expecting I would be getting a pair of nice new leather shoes with fancy buckles!' But they were a pleasing red and there was a little fancy stud on the uppers. And they were new, not second-hand!

On Monday morning Will showed me how to strike the steel caulkers on the tarmac road to make sparks which was great fun on the way to school. Les, in his shiny boots tried in vain to do the same but was disappointed. Will and I were so busy making sparks that we were late for school and Les had gone on ahead without us. Entering the class late I almost missed the register. Miss Benson sitting high in her desk, paused, her pen in her hand, nodded, and beckoned me forward. Clip-clop, clip-clop, clip-clop went my clogs on the wood-block floor, all the way past my teacher's desk, then on to mine, facing the whole class who stared goggle-eyed as they followed my noisy progress.

My face was as red as my clogs as the class whispered behind their hands and began tittering. One after the other they ducked down under their desks to scrutinise my footwear. I was so miserable I could hardly concentrate on my lessons. At playtime they chased me all over the playground, yelling, 'Clip-clop, clip-clop! Cloggy-dick, make them click!' Round and round they ran chanting the same silly rhyme over and over again. Then I heard Will shout from behind the railings that separated boys from girls. 'Leave her alone! Or I'll kick your bloody shins in!'

I could see his furious face jammed against the railings, and the girls retreated a little, but poked their tongues out at him. In class they made me feel like a leper. I ran home in tears. When I got in I flung the red clogs off.

'I hate them! I hate them! I hate the noise they make. And I hate being called Cloggy-dick by the other girls! No-one else wears clogs! Why should I?'

Dad put down his cup of tea and stared at me in astonishment and dismay. 'Nonsense! Everybody wears clogs where I come from!'

Clogs may have been familiar footwear in his home-town in Lancashire, but I didn't know anyone on Walney who wore them, certainly not any girl! Wearing them set me apart from the other children, and I hated being made a figure of fun. Firstly because of the boy's boots, now over the clogs that went clip-clop all over the place. Dad picked the little clogs up from the floor and turned them over in his square hands, his brown eyes screwed up thoughtfully.

Then his brow cleared and he took the clogs down to the lean-to where he had a bench. Still tearful, but full of curiosity, I followed him and watched him cut strips of leather from the tops of old boots. These he measured carefully along the clog irons. Next he prised the irons and their nails away from the wooden soles with his pinchers, leaving a line of holes in the wood. Afterwards he placed each clog on his 'last' and to my amazement, began to fill the holes left in the wood with spent matchsticks, and hammered them in. Finally, he laid the strips of leather neatly along the clog soles, and proceeded to cobble them on, carefully avoiding the filled-in nail-holes.

'There you are, try them on now, and see how quiet they are.'

Leaning back against the bench he watched me anxiously as I slipped my feet into them. On the concrete floor they just made a dull thudding noise which was better than clip-clop. I smiled dutifully and thanked him, for I appreciated that Dad was trying to help. But felt dubious all the same.

The next day at school instead of going clip-clop on the wood floor, they went clump-clump, clump-clump. The girls continued to call me Cloggy-dick and teased me as much as ever. They were still clogs and I hated them so much I wanted to be rid of them. Poor Dad was very disappointed when he saw I had gone back to wearing my old broken-down sandals which I had hidden under the couch after taking the boys' boots. But all the same, he still sympathised. A couple of weeks later he gave Mam the money and she bought me my very first pair of new shoes. Not with buckles as I had secretly hoped, but sensible school shoes, brogues I think they were. At home, and playing out, I still wore the red clogs to please Dad, and also to keep my new shoes looking smart. I would have hated him to think he had wasted his money buying the red clogs.

Chapter Ten

SCHOOL AND FRIENDS

Not all the girls at school were nasty to me. As well as my special friend Jenny, there was Elsie who lived in Dominion Street where her Mam had a small shop, and her Dad worked in the shipyard. She would invite me to her home when we finished school, and she would take me upstairs to play with her dolls. I went home with her several times, so I asked Mam if I could bring her home with me for a change, but Mam said 'no' quite firmly, adding sharply, 'I don't want you going home with anyone after school. There are jobs waiting to be done. The lads always arrive home on time, so I expect you to do the same.'

When I told Elsie what Mam had said she looked disappointed and never asked me home with her again, but began taking other girls home with her instead. She was an only child, so I expect she was lonely.

Jenny, my best friend, was a quiet, plain-faced girl except for her lovely brown eyes. Like me she was fond of reading, and out of the 2s she earned for working in the fish shop on Saturdays, her Mam bought her a girls' magazine, which she loved. She would sit with me in a corner of the playground telling me about the school stories that were in it. I became as engrossed with all the happenings as she was and pleaded with her to lend me the magazine over the weekend, until Monday morning.

I became so interested in the girls of 'Cliff House', 'Barbara Redfern' and her chums, her younger sister Doris, and Bessie Bunter, a silly fat girl who was always getting into scrapes who were all pupils at this 'posh' boarding school somewhere in the south of England, that I became convinced that it was a real school, and started writing letters to Barbara. I became keener on the magazine than Jenny, and couldn't wait for her to finish reading each new edition. After a few weeks went by without my receiving any replies to my letters I told Jenny how disappointed I was. She stared at me in amazement, her brown eyes wide, and began giggling.

'You didn't expect a reply, did you? It's not a real school, you silly ass. Fancy you, so good at reading and writing, not knowing that it was fiction just like our library books!'

I stared at her in embarrassment. 'But it seems so real, doesn't it, as though they were real girls like you and me.'

Jenny, who was more down-to-earth, nodded thoughtfully.

'Perhaps to the author they do seem real, as she has created them after all. Like the four girls in that book *Little Women*, that Miss Benson is reading out to us now.'

Each week on Friday afternoons after playtime, the teacher would read out to us a section of a book, and when she had reached the end of the story, we would have to write an essay on the story the following week. This was one of my favourite lessons at school, and I always received one of the best marks in the class for my essays. I suppose my love of reading and writing, and of school life, was what prompted me to write to 'Cliff House' School. But I still loved the magazine and looked forward to reading each week the latest adventures of 'Barbara & Co.' Jenny was a good-natured girl and didn't mind in the least sharing her precious magazine with me, her best friend since infant school.

When Ocean Road School had an open day each year, parents were invited to the school to inspect the classes where their children were taught. The pupils' best work in drawing and painting, essays and composition, would be pinned up on the walls and blackboard in a proud display for parents to inspect, and to chat to the teacher about their child's progress. How I used to envy those classmates whose parents came to the school!

Sadly for me, my parents never ever came. Dad had far too much to do all the time, but I suspect my mother was too lazy to get herself and the young ones ready for a walk down the lane and along Ocean Road to the school. I was so proud of my essays that were pinned up for all to see, yet I was bitterly disappointed that my own parents never saw any of my work or shared in my triumph. They were not the only parents who stayed away from the school – I expect for most of them, education was not on their minds. They were too enmeshed in their poverty, and worrying about where the next meal was coming from to consider that perhaps if their child was showing promise in any particular subject he or she could move up into higher education and have a better chance in life.

Many of them were not interested in higher education, so children weren't encouraged to enter the 11-plus examinations which enabled the children who passed to enter the grammar school. Of course the children of the 'better off' were encouraged to enter this all-important exam, not only by their parents, but by the teachers as well.

Ocean Road School had a very high standard. It was a really good school with excellent teachers who believed in stretching their pupils to the very best of their ability. To them, the poor clothes on pupils didn't matter. What was important to the teacher was the pupil's ability. They knew some of the better-off, but inferior scholars, succeeded in entering the grammar school because of their fathers' standing in the town. While the poorer, but cleverer ones whose parents wouldn't allow them to sit the 11-plus exam, and who therefore missed out on the grammar school education, had to be content with moving up to Ocean Road Secondary School, leaving school at fourteen years of age and ending up in some dead-end job.

Will wasn't in the least interested in sitting the 11-plus and going to grammar school when I asked him. 'Who wants to be like that toffee-nosed lot?' he asked scornfully.

He was more interested in 'passing his tenderfoot' and always had his nose in a dog-eared little book lent to him by one of his mates. They had joined the Scouts and Will was eager to do the same. Mam had managed to get him a second-hand scout uniform and he was thrilled to bits.

One day I sat with him on the front step of the caravan, while he wrestled with a length of rope Dad had given him for learning his knots. Dad, who had been weeding, came over to watch Will successfully do the knots to enable him to pass his 'tenderfoot test'. I watched in awe as he managed the reef knot, and its opposite, the granny knot. But somehow

Ocean Road School.

he couldn't manage the 'half-hitch' without Dad's help. I was always amazed at the things Dad could do. When he was laying the bricks in the kitchen in which to enclose Mam's new range I asked him how he could do so many things. He replied, with a cheerful grin, 'I'm a jack of all trades, but master of none.' I think he had tremendous enthusiasm for every job he tackled – be it carpentry, brick-laying, glazing, cobbling shoes, or gardening. Gardening, though, was his passion in which he excelled, getting great satisfaction from growing things from seed.

He had portioned off a corner at the bottom of the garden and told Mam to put all the potato and vegetable peelings in it. Before bringing in veggies for Mam to cook he would clean off the roots and outer leaves and pile them into 'the midden corner' to compost down for the garden. He also built a little square box with shafts and fitted old pram wheels on

Katie with her brother Les in the 1930s.

it, so that we had a little barrow in which to collect 'coddy-muck'(horse manure) to add to the midden for the garden. When he was working in his garden he was always aware of farmers with horses going down the lane, and when we came home from school he asked us if we had seen any 'coddy' on the road. Will or Les or myself would take the little barrow and a small shovel and walk along the lane looking for some of the golden-brown heaps which Dad valued so highly for growing his veggies. Sometimes we would go as far as Biggar Village and return in triumph with a barrow full, for which Dad would give a penny. I always put mine carefully away.

Mam and Dad were born in the late nineteenth century, and came from poor families, so had received very little education. We used to love

The cottage in Claddagh with Katie's grandfather and aunt outside.

to hear Mam talking about Galway on the west coast of Ireland, when we were children. Mam's father, our Irish grandfather, had like many other young Irishmen sailed over to Boston, Massachusetts, to seek his fortune. He begged his girlfriend to go with him but she wouldn't leave her parents. He came back several times pleading with her, and when she still refused, he finally came back to Galway, and they got married, and settled down.

With his savings he bought a small thatched cottage in the fishing village known as the Claddagh, Galway, and a small fishing boat, a 'Hooker'. There he began to earn his living fishing in Galway Bay. Mam said it was a very hard life. The fishermen's wives used to stand waiting at Claddagh quay for the hookers to return with the catch. The women used to sell the fish while the men looked after their boats' maintenance and repaired fishing nets. The wives kept some of the fish, salted it down then buried it in the earth beside their cottage to feed their families. There were no pantries, just a small cupboard, and certainly no refrigerators then. The wives who sold the fish also handled the money to pay out for necessities such as a few groceries.

But fishing was a very poor living, depending on the catch, and Mam said they often starved. They were so famished, she told us, that one day her sister Kate grabbed a chicken that had strayed from someone's hen-coop. Without hesitation she wrung its neck, hid the chicken under her shawl, and hurried to the nearby beach of Salthill, where she plucked its feathers then buried them in the sand. Hiding it again under her shawl she hurried home and gave it to her mother to clean and cook. The family had their first meal for days. Being Catholics, her parents scolded her severely for stealing, and told her she must accompany them to Confession, and ask the priest for forgiveness. She said she had often wondered what their life would have been like if only her mother, Bridget, had agreed to join her father, Morgan, in Boston. They most certainly would have been better off and she and her brothers and sisters would have been Americans. I considered her life had been a hard one in her childhood, and continued to be hard now.

We enjoyed Mam talking about her life in Galway, how as children she and her brothers and sisters played on the beach at Salthill, in the same way as we ourselves loved playing on the shore at Biggar Bank. How when they grew up the First World War had broken out between Germany and England, and because Ireland was ruled by England three of her brothers volunteered to fight the Kaiser. Dominic and Michael went into the Connaught Rangers, an Irish regiment, and Patrick into the Royal Navy. Her eldest brother Thomas stayed in Galway and worked with their father on his fishing trips. Mam herself went over to England in 1912 to work in a hotel in Cambridge, but returned to Galway at the outbreak of war.

Sadly two of her brothers died in the war. Dominic was killed in the first Battle of the Somme, and Patrick died with pneumonia on board ship and was buried in Liverpool. Meanwhile in 1915 Mam was recruited with a group of Irish girls and brought over to Barrow to work on munitions in Vickers. Her other brother Michael returned from the trenches, too broken in body and spirit to settle down again to resume working with his father and brother Thomas on the fishing trips. Instead, he became a 'gentleman of the road' – a tramp.

Chapter Eleven

A GUIDE AT LAST!

D ad didn't talk as much about his family as Mam did about hers, but it seemed his mother was a lovely-looking woman, who was heartbroken when her son, Arthur James, was drowned in the River Ribble. The poor lad was only sixteen years old. Dad must have been about four years old at the time. He had another older brother, John, and two older sisters, and one younger sister. Dad said they were very poor. His father worked down the coal mine, but he drank most of his wages. In those Victorian days when young boys of six years old went down the mine, Dad did so as well to earn a few pennies to help his mother buy some food. He had not had much schooling. He said you had to have a penny each day to go to school. If there wasn't a penny available, he had to stay at home. But Dad had an enquiring mind and in spite of his lack of years of schooling he was observant and picked things up very quickly. He liked tackling the big crossword in the Sunday paper, and I used to enjoy helping by suggesting different answers. He was interested in words and their meanings, and this was probably why he could write a surprisingly good letter.

With both my parents being away from their families we never knew any grandparents, aunts or cousins. I envied the girls I knew at school who had cousins, who were also their playmates. They joined the Brownies together, went to dancing classes and went to music lessons to learn to play the piano or the violin. As these girls grew older they planned to join the Girl Guides, which I was longing to join.

By now Will, who was in his first year at Ocean Road Secondary, was also a very keen, fully-fledged Scout. He was especially excited when they would all go away camping. Often it was only somewhere

Katie in the 1930s wearing one of her brother's Navy hats.

on Biggar Bank, but this fed Will's sense of adventure, being away from home, erecting the tents and helping to make the meals, and enjoying the jolly sing-songs around the camp fire at night. But on other occasions the troop would go away to somewhere into the Lake District, such as Coniston, for a weekend. There they would do lots of walking, and Will would bring back fir cones and stick them on the mantelpiece, telling us how wonderful the trees and scenery was, all lovely lakes and fells, not flat and treeless like Walney Island. I was green with envy and wished so much that I would be able to do what he was doing. I begged Mam to let me join the Girl Guides, but she flatly refused.

My life was very unhappy at that time. I dearly wanted to sit for the 11-plus exam which if I passed successfully would enable me to enter the grammar school, and if I was good enough, follow my dream of becoming an English teacher. Dad flatly refused to allow me to sit for the exam, and would not even discuss the matter. He failed to see anything wrong with the secondary school which Will was attending, and by now in his fifties, Dad was horrified at the thought of all the expenditure of grammar school uniforms and hockey sticks and other paraphernalia that higher education demanded.

At school my teacher was very disappointed on hearing this news, and spoke to me at length on the subject, pointing out the advantages. Other girls in my class who were lesser scholars, but better off financially, were certainly going to try for it. Miserable and unhappy, I was too embarrassed to explain to the teacher that my parents were only interested in their three eldest children attending secondary school and leaving at fourteen years of age to take up employment, and therefore to ease their burden of bringing up the three younger ones. Will, whose sense of adventure was awakened by his joining the Boy Scouts was already talking about joining the Royal Navy when he was old enough.

I was disappointed and wretched about not going to the grammar school. I grieved to myself that it seemed as though I was never going to be allowed to do anything I wanted. I had to accept that my father felt he was unable to afford the school expenses of the grammar school, but what about the Girl Guides? That was not going to cost much. Dad had no objection to Will joining the Scouts – indeed he seemed to relish hearing about his exploits, as did Mam. All through my junior school years I had envied better-off girls who went to dancing classes, or the Brownies, or were learning to play piano. I was too old now for Brownies, but eligible to join the Girl Guides if only I got the chance. From then on I began to pester my mother about it. How she must have hated me. Her excuse was that she needed me, that she had a difficult baby to deal with, and depended on my returning home from school each day to give her a much needed respite from the crying child.

To add to my disappointment about not going to the grammar school was the knowledge that Irene Albion was starting there. I was frankly envious when, on my first day walking to Ocean Road Secondary, I saw her by the tram stop, proudly wearing her new grammar school uniform and with a new satchel at her feet. I felt too choked to call over to her, and just gave her a brief wave, and hurried on along towards Ocean Road Secondary. My resentment against my father for not allowing me to sit the exam deepened, and turned to anger. Irene's father was younger than Dad, but he too was on the dole, though they only had two children. He had allowed Irene to sit the exam, but my Dad would not even listen to my pleas. In his mind girls had no need of further education, they got married. His attitude changed the whole course of my life.

However, I was agreeably surprised with my advent into my 'new' school, and was delighted to find I was assigned to 1A because of my excellent record in the junior school. Some of my old classmates were in it too, which pleased me enormously.

The teachers were excellent, encouraging us to work earnestly on our subjects, and strive as hard as we had done previously in the primary school. The history teacher was called Mr Gamble, and he used to make us laugh. However, he wouldn't tolerate any slacking, or talking in class. Will told me that once when he was talking to the boy behind him, Mr Gamble threw a well-aimed piece of chalk at Will's head. Will turned around at once. Mr Gamble warned, 'Next time, I'll throw my desk!'

The whole class roared with laughter, Will included.

Will was always a bit mischievous and was more interested in his mates than serious study. Mr Gamble began to call him 'Lord Useless Percy'. At the time there was a politician in the government called Lord Eustace Percy. Mr Gamble was very popular with a great sense of humour, and was an excellent history teacher.

The Geography teacher was Mr Satterthwaite, and the English teacher was a Miss Benson, though no relation to the other Miss Benson in the primary. These three teachers were the most important to me. I forget the name of the science teacher, and the one who taught us in the domestic science class.

Altogether it seemed I was going to enjoy being in secondary school after all. But that was before I began to be taught maths. In the primary school this was known as arithmetic, where I managed quite well with long division, sums, and multiplication. I knew my times tables and, though arithmetic was not my favourite subject, I did moderately well.

Now however, in the secondary, it was mathematics, which I came to dread. I think I took a dislike to the teacher, Mr Park from the beginning. He frightened me to death. He had black hair that shone like patent leather and was brushed back from a forehead that contained two bumps that I imagined were the beginning of two horns, like the devil. He was clean-shaven but always had a blue chin, as though there was a blue beard fighting to come through. His dark blue eyes behind black horn-rimmed glasses were cold and hard. He was immaculately suited, dapper even, compared to the other male teachers, who favoured tweedy jackets and corduroy trousers. But there was something cold about Mr Park that repelled me. He certainly lacked the other teachers' warmth, charm, and humour, for I never ever saw him smile, or make us laugh as did Mr Gamble.

I considered mathematics to be a cold, unfeeling subject, which gave me no joy at all. Perhaps Mr Park felt none in teaching his subject either. Maybe I was so busy studying him when he was explaining about Pythagoras' theorem; this first lesson went right over my head. Maybe he knew this for he would fire a question at me that I couldn't answer. Something about 'Pie' equalling something or other. The only 'pie' I was familiar with was the pie I had made in cookery class. If I had taken in the first few sessions in his class, perhaps I would have done much better. Also if I had warmed to Mr Park in the first place, I would not have had such consistently low marks in mathematics, compared to my high marks in English, history and geography. Science was not one of my favourite subjects, but I still did my best.

However, in spite of my weakness in maths, my strength in the other subjects took me safely through into 2a and on into 3a in 1934, my last year, which by the time December came I would be fourteen years old and would have to leave. I could not bear the thought of that so pushed it away to the back of my mind and concentrated on my lessons and the friendship of some of the girls who shared my interests.

In the meantime there were other exciting things to enjoy. When I was thirteen years old I was given the chance, at last, to join the Girl Guides. One of my classmates, Lily, told me that she was leaving the Girl Guides and hoping to join the Sea Cadets, and said she would sell me her Guide uniform for 4s. I was thrilled to bits and promptly gave her some pennies I had saved by running errands, and which I had hidden in a corner of my old satchel. That night when I eagerly told Mam about the uniform she laughed shrilly, demanding to know where she was going to get 4s. Mam had a secret little hoard screwed up in an old stocking under the mattress, from pennies we had given her earned from running messages, but didn't know that I had seen where she hid the hoard. She probably used this money for her little forays on the second-hand stalls in Barrow market. She was furious when I told her I had already given Lily some pennies, and in future, instead of giving pennies I had earned to her, I would save them for Lily for the uniform. Angrily, she aimed a swipe at me with the wet dishcloth she was using. I certainly knew how to get on the wrong side of her. I quickly made amends by putting baby Ally in the pram, sneaking my library book under the cover, and pushing the pram down the garden path to the lane outside. I hoped by the time I got back she would have recovered her normal composure, and accepted my longing to join the Guides.

Eileen, or Ally, as six-year-old Evelyn called her, turned out to be my mother's last baby, and was a troublesome and restless child from the start, always crying and wearing out my mother, who must have been in her mid-forties at the time. Mam said the baby had been 'scriking' (Irish for crying) all day, but the funny thing was that as soon as I began wheeling the pram in the lane she fell asleep. I wondered why Mam never thought of taking her out in the pram herself. She could have gone to the village to see Maud instead of her coming to visit us. As I walked the thought came to me that if I took the baby out every day when I came home from school, walking the pram to Biggar Bank, I could sit in one of the shelters facing the sea and read to my heart's content, while the sea air would be good for the sleeping baby.

When this became my new daily routine after school, my mother was relieved, though suspicious of my sudden willingness to mind my baby sister, but was agreeable at last to my joining the Guides, and when I brought the uniform home she admitted grudgingly that it was a good fit. But things were not as rosy as they appeared. There were new battles ahead. When it was Guides night there was always a scene about letting me go to St Mary's Hall near the promenade, and she told me firmly that going camping was out of the question because I was needed at home. I argued that Will was always allowed to go to camp and to Scout meetings, so why couldn't I? I still followed my routine after school of pushing the pram to the shelter on Biggar Bank, but took my Guides book with me and learned from it how to pass my tenderfoot, and using the same bit of rope as Will, learned how to do my knots.

When the night of my tenderfoot test came I hurried home from school and eagerly slipped on my uniform while eating a slice of bread and jam. My mother immediately stopped me going out of the door and pointed to the pram in which she had placed the baby.

'Guides or no Guides', she said firmly, 'Ally has to be taken out as usual.'

'Please, Mam,' I pleaded, 'I mustn't miss tonight, it's my tenderfoot test!'

But Mam was already pushing the pram down the step and took no notice of my distress. I followed, and grabbing the pram handle shouted furiously, 'Alright then! I'll damn well take her with me to the Guides!'

Her mocking laughter followed me down the path causing Dad to look up from his weeding. He grinned at the sight of his daughter in her Guide uniform angrily pushing the pram, and guessed there had been another battle, which Mam had won this time.

Chapter Twelve

OFF TO THE LAKES

My parents lived simple lives, with little pleasures such as the Sunday newspaper, but sometimes on Saturday night Dad would go up to the Queen's Hotel, the village pub, and would bring back a bottle of Guinness for Mam which she enjoyed. One Saturday, when there was going to be a free hotpot supper for customers at the Queen's, Dad took Mam with him for a change and she was delighted. I stayed home to put the younger ones to bed – and do some reading. Will and Les went to Biggar Bank to join other lads in a simple game of cricket.

When the proprietor from the Queen's was passing sometimes, she would stop her little Austin car outside our gate in the lane and come to speak to Dad about his garden produce. Sometimes she would buy a cauliflower and some lettuces, and when she noticed we had some ducklings she asked him if he would sell her a couple of them for her to cook for her clients. She had a tearoom built on to the old inn, and served excellent meals. This bit of extra money was very useful to Dad, who being a gardener, always had his eye on the next spring planting. He often had a surplus of vegetables, so would dig some up and lay them out neatly on his flat cart. Then he would set off for Vickerstown to try to sell them to the shops there. However, there were many allotments on Ocean Road, and the holders were also selling their produce to the shops, but Dad knew most of them and joined in friendly chats with these other gardeners and they all enjoyed discussing their produce, and selling where they could.

A trip had been arranged by the Guides, and a week before the Lakes weekend, I plucked up the courage to tell Mam I would be going away

Katie on Lake Windermere (at Ambleside) in the 1930s.

with the Guides on the Saturday. Dad came in with me, to give his support. My Mam shook her head firmly. 'No! You'll need money for the coach which I haven't got to give you.'

'I've already paid the money for the coach and my food, Mam. It's all arranged for me to go this coming weekend, so you can't stop me.'

She glared at me angrily, ready to put her foot down.

But Dad intervened and said said soothingly, 'Let her go, Mary, she's a good lass and helps you a lot. It'll do her good to get away, and it's only one night!'

Mam was furious with me and turned on Dad angrily. 'But it's all day Saturday and most of Sunday. Ally is teething and her crying is driving me mad. Also with Will being away, Les has to do extra jobs. She's needed here, Bill!'

Katie's brother Les in his Navy days.

In the end, however, she had to give in, and even said she hoped I would enjoy it as much as Will had always done, and for that I was grateful.

On a lovely July day, the coach swept us along leafy Abbey Road, the main road out of the town, to the little village of Dalton, and on through gently undulating green countryside to the ancient market town of Ulverston. I could hardly contain my excitement as I caught glimpses of the Lancashire fells. Arriving at Newby Bridge I could see the beginnings of Lake Windermere. The road wound through a wonderful canopy of thousands of lush green trees, following the contours of the lake which was widening before my awestruck eyes, the adjacent fells on the opposite side creating shimmering images on the rippling blue water.

The coach slowed as we reached Bowness-on-Windermere, giving us all a chance to gaze on this lovely scene. An elegant white steamer waited by the pier, and another one was beginning its journey through the glittering water, passing Belle Isle with its unusual round house built in 1774. Huge hotels straddled the hillsides commanding splendid views over the water to the opposite side of the lake, to Sawrey and the distant Old Man of Coniston, as the fell was called. On again the coach travelled uphill and down beside the ever-widening lake, leaving it again as the road took us through the small town of Windermere, and on again along the road to Ambleside. This small village situated at the end of Lake Windermere with its houses and hotels mainly built of the local stone and slate, had wonderful views of the distant Langdale Pikes. Leaving the lake behind us we soon came to the small lake called Rydal Water, then on to Grasmere, our destination.

The coach left the road before reaching this village, and entered a huge field not far from Grasmere Lake. Following Miss Wray, our Guide Captain, out of the coach, we came to a standstill awaiting her instructions. She told us a local farmer, who owned the field, was allowing us the use of his barn, a short walk away, but in the meantime we could sit down and eat the sandwiches and drink the cold tea we had brought with us. But dinner that night was to be a hotpot supper we had paid for and would be at the farmhouse.

Afterwards she led us on a walk through the village of Grasmere, where we enjoyed looking into the quaint shops, and buying samples of gingerbread from a tiny shop where it was made. Next we went to Grasmere Church and stood around the grave of William Wordsworth, the most famous of the Lake Poets. At Ocean Road School we were all familiar with their work, as poetry was a regular part of our English lessons, which I enjoyed. I was so glad I had been given the opportunity to visit the final resting place of Wordsworth and his family.

I was so entranced by the beautiful scenery around me I just wanted to stand and stare, to breathe in the scents of the many gorgeous trees. I revelled in admiring the ever-changing colours of the fells, watching the way clouds drifted slowly by, casting their shadows on the sides of the valleys. I gazed at the fells' reflections in the lake they surrounded. No need to wonder, then, why so many writers and painters were drawn to this magical place to record their impressions in words and paint. I understood why so many visitors enjoyed walking around the attractive Lakeland villages in the same way as we had enjoyed Grasmere.

Later on we went for a very interesting walk around Grasmere Lake with our captain leading. A senior Guide trained in first aid, stayed in the middle of the line while another senior first-aider stayed at the rear to keep a watch on those like me who kept stopping to stare across the lake at the scenery and drink everything in. Though it was level for most of the way, there were some stony areas on the path and some rather wet ones too, so care was needed, for it would have been quite easy to slip and sustain some nasty cuts and bruises. However, it all ended happily with no mishaps, but feeling hungry, and looking forward to our supper, we trooped over to the farm where the farmer's wife had made a huge hotpot for us, which we thoroughly enjoyed together with big mugs of tea, and homemade fruit cake to follow. Our wonderful day ended with a sing-song in the barn before we bedded down on the sweet-smelling straw to sleep.

The next morning we had a brisk walk before returning to the farmhouse for a hearty breakfast of milky porridge, toast and mugs of tea, and afterwards thanking our hosts and bidding them farewell. Then another brisk walk took us back to the field and the waiting coach, and the journey home. It all seemed to end too quickly for me and I was very sorry to leave the magical and beautiful Lake District, but hoped that there would be other visits to look forward to. Some day, I vowed to myself, when I am grown up, I shall come back – not just for a day, but to find a job and stay for a long time, to enjoy living here.

Though feeling down that my wonderful weekend spent in such scenic surroundings among beautiful trees was over so quickly, and I was back on bare, windy Walney Island, I dutifully placed my souvenirs of fir

A modern view across the gullies from Carr Lane.

cones on the mantelpiece next to Will's, and was rewarded with a warm smile from Mam, who was obviously relieved to see me back again. She was missing Will a lot. Having left school on reaching fourteen years of age the previous year, he had found the only job he could get was 'living-in', working on a farm at Cartmel. He had to give up attending Scout meetings which upset him very much. In his letters he told Mam and Dad that he hated working on the farm, but was still hoping that as soon as he was old enough he would join the Royal Navy. My younger brother, Les, who was now in his first year in the secondary school, was also interested in joining the Navy.

My final year at Ocean Road Secondary, 1934, was passing all too quickly and the girls in my year, 3a, were all wondering what awaited them in the world of work. From what Will had said there were very few jobs to be had in Barrow. For the first time since beginning at the secondary, I began regretting again that I had not been given the chance to go to the grammar school. Perhaps by this stage, I fretted, I would be working towards a place at a college or even university. Whereas now, at the end of the year upon leaving school at fourteen I had no idea what would be waiting for me.

My friend Jenny who would also be leaving at the end of the year told me gloomily that her uncle Walter wanted her to work full-time in his wet-fish shop, telling her she was very lucky to be able to drop into a job that was waiting for her. She hated the smell of fish and was not looking forward to that at all. Some of the girls in our year suggested there might be office jobs available in Vickers shipyard in the personnel department, perhaps as clerks or tracers. Some of the girls wrote in about clerks' jobs, Jenny and I applied for positions as 'lady tracers' without really knowing what this entailed. Vickers, however, in their reply said they were only interested in girls who were receiving a grammar school education. For those of us who had wanted to go to the grammar, this was a very bitter pill indeed to have to swallow, and to wonder what the future held.

Chapter Thirteen

THE QUEEN'S AT BIGGAR

A few weeks later, I was steadily making my way along the lane, with my satchel bulging with books, when a car stopped. The driver was the proprietor of the Queen's Hotel at Biggar. She raised a gloved hand, and beckoned me forward. I was puzzled as to why she wanted to speak to me. She had passed me many times in her car before, without showing any interest in me, even though I had passed close to her when she was talking to Dad at the gate about his garden produce.

When I approached the car I saw she was looking me up and down with narrowed eyes, like a farmer studying the quality of the cattle at market. I felt uneasy under this steady scrutiny, which reminded me of the story of Hansel and Gretel where the witch was planning to eat the children; and I wondered if she too, was a witch, and giggled to myself. But I quickly composed myself and waited for her to speak. She asked sharply, 'Katie Percy? How old are you now?'

'I'll be fourteen in a few months' time, a couple of weeks before Christmas.'

Her hard, shrewd eyes, yellow like a tiger's, raked my face. 'What about working for me this weekend, Friday after school until Sunday? I'll pay you 2s.'

I caught my breath in excitement. A whole 2s, which I could save for more guide outings to the Lakes. 'Yes, thank you, I'll come.'

She nodded briefly and drove off towards the village. Elated, I hurried on home eager to tell my news. Mam was busy ironing as I burst into the kitchen.

'Mam! What do you think? That lady from the pub in the village wants me to go there to work for her this weekend!'

Katie aged seventeen.

'Well I never!' Mam declared. She laid down the flat iron and stared at me in surprise. She jerked her head towards the satchel of books, and said scathingly, 'You'll not have time to stick your nose in them.'

I gaped at my mother for a second and swallowed in dismay. A whole weekend without reading time had not occurred to me at all.

'But I will have the evenings after school for reading, at least.'

'But you will still have to take Ally out, don't forget!' my mother warned.

She picked up the iron again and thumped it down on the garment with satisfaction.

The next morning at school I was eager to tell Jenny that I had been offered a job.

'That hotel in the village, you mean? I went there once with Uncle Walter who was delivering some fish. It's a nice place inside, cosy and seventeenth-century I think. Have you never been to it?'

I shook my head. 'Not to the Queen's, but we went to visit Maud, Mam's friend, in her cottage in the village a few years ago.'

Jenny sighed. 'Wish it was me. Be better than working in a fish shop, you lucky thing.'

Neither Jenny nor I had an idea just then what I had let myself in for.

The next day, Friday, I rushed home from school in a state of great excitement. Mam had a few things ready in a bass bag, my nightdress, a toothbrush and a couple of her worn aprons. They were so well-washed the pattern in the cotton material had almost disappeared, but they were very clean and well ironed. Mam had been a laundress and her washing and ironing was immaculate.

'I wonder what work I'll have to do, Mam?'

My mother shrugged carelessly. It seemed to me that she did not care what I did, so long as I was going to earn some money for her. It was very disappointing. 'You'll know soon enough, just do as you're told, and learn all you can!'

She handed me a cup of tea with some jam sandwiches.

I glanced hungrily at the big iron pot bubbling away on the stove. 'Is there no dinner for me?'

'Mrs Black will give you something, I'm sure. She's got full and plenty. It's only a small hotel but she does meals as well.'

Not too happy about missing my dinner, I hoped she was right. Hurrying forwards along the lane, I saw the sea-wall protecting the village come into view. To me, Biggar looked more like an ancient fort than a village. Its odd construction gave the impression that a pile of cobblestones, flung up by an angry sea, had somehow settled into a huddle of tiny cottages and farms. The residents were farming land their grandfathers had been born on when Barrow was a mere fishing village. The distant iron forest of shipyard cranes across the tidal grey water of the channel was of little importance to them.

I hurried towards the hoarding on a high hedge which stated it was the Queen's Arms Hotel. Eagerly I turned into its cobbled yard, passing an old barn and outbuildings which suggested it had been a farm in earlier times. The Queen's was a long, low white building dominated by a massive central chimney of some antiquity. The small windows of square panes were adorned with boxes of red geraniums on the ledges, providing vivid splashes of colour against the white walls. An old barn

The Queen's Arms in Biggar Village.

had been incorporated into the original building for a tea-room, forming the whole into a pleasing L-shape.

The heavy oak door stood open. Rather nervously I walked into the small entrance which faced a large room containing a wealth of oak beams and slate-flagged floors, and slowly gazed around. The inside walls were also painted white, the red curtains, gaily decorated with hunting scenes, which together with the red geraniums, created a vivid contrast. The room was filled with dark antique furniture, and a huge open fire straddled a large whitened hearth, upon which there was a plethora of brass warming pans, pokers, tongs and coal scuttles reflecting the glow from the blazing logs. I caught my breath, enchanted with the old oak settles, cosily placed each side of the fireplace, and admired their long red cushions of hunting scenes that matched the curtains. The refectory and other tables gleamed with the patina of old age and vigorous polishing. There was so much for me to take in, for I had never seen such a place before, or so much pewter and brass in my life. For a moment it was as though I had been transported back into another century. Transfixed, I stared in awe at the face of an old grandfather clock chiming the hour of five. I shivered suddenly without knowing why. From the distance came the clattering of dishes and I could smell food, bringing me back to the present.

'Follow me. I'll show you your room!'

The sharp voice of Mrs Black, who had suddenly appeared before me, made me jump and meekly, I followed. We passed through an old door climbing a winding staircase, its wooden boards whispering their knowledge of those who had come and gone down the years. The place was alive with atmosphere, the air filled with the indefinable smell of warm seasoned timber mingling with the faint aroma of beer. Excitement surged in me as I followed the aloof figure along a gloomy passage, and I glanced over my shoulder murmuring to her about ghosts.

My new mistress, however, had no time for such fancies, and ignored my shy attempts at conversation, making it clear that I was an insignificant person, brought in only to work. She paused on the landing.

'Put your things in there.' She pointed to a small room containing a wardrobe, chest of drawers, and a small bed in which I was to sleep, and waited while I took my nightdress and toothbrush out of the bag and placed them in one of the drawers with one of the aprons. The other I hurriedly slipped over my cotton dress. Then she led me downstairs again into the room I admired so much.

We passed the old clock, turned, and went along another passage which contained the scullery and pantry, to the big working kitchen. On one wall was a vast black range where she did all the cooking. Facing it was a huge well-scrubbed table. Two smaller tables, piled with soiled crockery, stood under a window. At the other end of the kitchen was an old sofa and chair under another window, and in a corner stood a squat little boiler which kept the hotel supplied with hot water. Along the walls were large cupboards with sliding doors containing good quality crockery, and the wooden floor was as well-scrubbed as the table.

A buxom girl of about twenty was energetically washing up at the deep sink. She turned when Mrs Black addressed her.

'Bessie, this is Katie. Keep her busy, and give her something to eat.'

Bessie gave me a warm, friendly smile as Mrs Black thrust a tea towel into my hand, before stalking off and leaving us to it.

Bessie, up to her elbows in hot water, washed the dishes and I dried them and piled them onto the big table until Bessie showed me where they went in the cupboards. Afterwards she went into the pantry which was facing the scullery and cut up ham and bread and made me some lovely sandwiches to be eaten with a glass of milk. While I ate, she brought out polish and cloths from the scullery cupboard and set them on the table next to the silver.

'Now that the silver things have been washed, they have to be polished.'

There were piles of silver; teapots, milk jugs, sugar bowls, and lots of cutlery. I stared in dismay. 'All of this to be polished?'

Bessie sighed ruefully, and nodded towards the tearoom.

'I've been run off my feet waiting on for the afternoon teas. When it's nice weather like this we get a lot of customers, who, with it being August are on holiday. Mind you! I got a few nice tips today!'

She thrust her hand into her apron pocket and brought out a handful of coins which she piled on the table. They were mostly threepenny bits and a couple of sixpences. Counting them expertly, she nodded with satisfaction. 'That's 3s! Not bad!' She reached onto the window-sill to where there stood a George V Coronation mug, in which she saved her tips, and dropped the money into it. 'Most days, I only get a few pennies. Depends on how busy we are. By the end of the week tips help to boost my wages up a bit.'

I glanced at her admiringly. 'Sounds like awfully hard work! First of all running in and out with these trays, then the washing up, and

Katie with a feline companion.

cleaning this silver afterwards, all on your own? Phew! You certainly deserve those tips!'

'That's why she brought you in to help,' said Bessie. 'It's not so bad for two people.'

'It's still a lot of work though.' I said.

I took the yellow polishing cloth she handed to me and watched Bessie begin applying a little polish vigorously to the milk jugs, sugar bowls, and teapots, and I rubbed them with the polishing cloth. Bessie, a well-built, strong girl with plump rosy cheeks, dark eyes and curly black hair, worked quickly, obviously used to this work, while after a bit of feverish rubbing I tired, finding polishing so boring, and wishing it was all done.

Later, to my dismay, Bessie laid down the polishing things and went over to the sink to wash her hands.

'Sorry Katie, I have to leave you, to serve in the bar. Don't look so downhearted, we all have to learn.'

With an encouraging smile she whirled out of the kitchen to the bar. I could hear the clump of boots, and the scraping back of chairs as a noisy game of darts got under way. I peeped out and saw the room I had admired earlier filling up with farmers and their labourers.

I began again, without a grreat dea of enthusiasm, and was still plodding on when Mrs Black bounced in to inspect my work. 'You are using far too much polish!' she commented tartly. 'Try using some elbow grease!' and bounced out again. She had this habit of suddenly appearing from nowhere like an evil genie which I was beginning to dislike. I picked up the cloth and rubbing harder did the whole lot again, and had to admit to myself that there was an improvement, which gave me a small satisfaction as I put them all away in the silver cupboard.

I was feeling very tired after my new labours and sat down on the old sofa and dozed off to sleep. I was awakened around ten o'clock by a tall, dark-haired man, whom I presumed was Mr Black. He handed me some warm milk, his brown eyes kind as he smiled down at me.

'Little girls like you should be in bed!'

On Saturday morning I was awakened by Bessie at five o'clock. In the light of a candle I saw her put a warning finger to her lips. 'Be as quiet as you can! We don't want *her* up!'

She slithered away, an amorphous shadow in the flickering light of the candle, silent as a cat in her stockinged feet. I dragged my unwilling body out of bed, yawned, and began dressing. Later, as I tiptoed cautiously along the dim passage with the boards creaking alarmingly, I realised Bessie had acquired the skill of avoiding the noisy ones.

In the kitchen she was creeping about like a burglar, preparing a pot of tea. She held a warning finger to her lips, and whispered.

'She doesn't allow us tea, but we need something to wake us up, so blow her.'

I was warming to the kindly Bessie more and more, and the lovely tea was most welcome, she was an ally in the enemy camp. Mr Black seemed nice though, but Bessie had told me when we were working together the previous evening, that he went off to the shipyard at seven each morning so was only there of an evening. The hotel was very much the concern of Mrs Black, and in her name.

Moving quietly Bessie removed the signs of our illicit tea, then tiptoeing into the scullery opposite the pantry she opened the door of the cleaning cupboard. Arming us both with black-lead and brushes, buckets, cloths, hearth-stone, polish and dusters, she outlined the routine.

The amount of work was appalling. She led me into the big room she said was known as the 'farm' kitchen, which Mrs Black had ordered her to get me to clean, telling me to start first by cleaning and laying the fireplace, next washing and whitening the hearth, polishing the furniture, cleaning the brasses, then lastly scrubbing the flagged floor. She would be cleaning the two bar rooms close by. Finally she reminded me that Mrs Black came down at eight o'clock and with an encouraging smile left to make a start on her own work.

After she had gone I stood staring with sinking heart at the mess left by the evening's revellers, and thought back to my delight of the first sight of this room yesterday. Now in the cold light of morning I saw nothing romantic about dead ashes spilling over a once-white hearth, or over-flowing ashtrays scattered on tables sticky with beer, and dried cow-dung clinging to chair legs and rungs.

Behind me the old clock slyly reminded the time was now half-past five, and Bessie's warning came back to me.

'She comes down at eight. God help us!'

A wave of fear swept over me, and as though to add to my misery, a cloud of soot slid down the wide chimney, covering absolutely everything. Steady sounds of activity from Bessie's end spurred me into action. Feverishly, I attacked the ashes and laid paper and sticks

Inside the Queen's in recent years when Katie returned to Walney.

in the iron 'basket' and began black-leading. In my anxiety to get the loathsome task over quickly, I banged my knuckles so often on the cast-iron basket they began to bleed, and I got the hideous black stuff all over me. But I had forgotten the chimney sides. I began to sweep them with frantic haste. I was soon enveloped in soot, as well as the fireplace I had just cleaned. Dismayed, I began the cleaning again. I felt like one of the little chimneysweeps in Charles Dickens' stories, but blinking back the tears, got busy washing and whitening the hearth.

There was still the furniture to polish, and I stood gazing with distaste at the dirty, overflowing ash-trays, trying to remember what Bessie had said I had to do next. Oh yes, empty the ash-trays, wash the sticky beer stains then polish the tables. My bucket of water was dirty, so I rushed into the scullery, emptied out the bucket in the sink, and refilled the bucket with more hot water to wash the tables. While the bucket was filling, I caught sight of my face in the small mirror that hung over the sink. My brown hair, powdered with soot, was clinging damply around my face which was also streaked with soot, amid a few tearstains. If I had not felt so wretched I would have laughed at the spectacle I made. What would Jenny say if she saw me like this? I pictured her in her Uncle Walter's fish shop wearing a white apron as she stood behind the counter, her hands blue with cold as she handled the fish. I reflected better hands blue with cold, than filthy and stained by black-lead; at that moment her job seemed far preferable to mine.

Sighing, I turned off the tap and lugged the bucket back to the 'farm' kitchen and began to wash the tables and dirty ash-trays. Later, starting on the furniture, I applied polish lavishly to everything, but rub as I might I could not impart the mirror-like sheen I had so admired yesterday. The flagged floor I was sure, would be easy, I often washed the floor for Mam, but this floor was much bigger, so I tackled it with wide confident sweeps, only to find in order to dry the patches I had to scrabble back and forth to the bucket. The result was an interesting pattern of tide-lines all over the floor and wet sooty skirts clinging to my legs. There was still the brass – a whole foundry of it. By the time I had finished, I ached in muscles I never knew I had. Despite my labours the room looked an absolute mess, the furniture dull and greasy, the brasses streaked with white polish. I also looked a mess. I felt thoroughly dirty and was very, very hungry.

I was just going to look for Bessie when the clock struck eight, the stair door flew open and out popped Mrs Black, just like the bird in a cuckoo clock. Though this was no shy cuckoo, she was more like an enraged magpie. She stared around in horror, and flew across the room at me with yellow eyes blazing. Her claws went poking onto the mantelpiece which was thick with soot, and gazing around the room she screeched, 'Oh! My lovely furniture! You stupid girl! Don't you know anything?'

I stood rooted to the spot with fear, struck dumb by the rage on her red face, and in her voice. She wasn't a big woman but she terrified me. The next hour was a nightmare. She brought warm water and vinegar and pushed me to the tables to wash all the surplus polish off their surfaces. If she had stood over me with a whip I could not have been more frightened. I trembled in every limb, my hands shaking so much I could hardly hold the cloth. She made me do everything again, even the floor, ranting at me the whole time.

'Scrub small patches, use a bit of elbow grease and less soap. Get into the corners girl, anyone can do middles!'

It was her signature tune which I was to hear all weekend and she did not let up until I had done the last patch of floor. Then she turned abruptly and marched off into the kitchen, leaving me gripping the table nearest to me to stop myself from shaking. I felt like I had been forced through a mangle which had squeezed every bit of life out of me, then, as hollow as a husk of corn, I had been picked up by a whirlwind and swirled about until I felt dizzy. A few minutes later the delicious smell of home-cured bacon sizzling in the pan wafted into my nostrils. This enticing smell of food brought me back to life.

Bessie, who must have heard Mrs Black's sharp bullying voice, came through from the snug carrying her bucket. She gave me a fierce little hug in sympathy.

'Come on, let's empty the buckets, and wash our hands in the scullery.'

Then Mrs Black called out briefly.

'Breakfast's ready.'

Katie aged twenty-eight.

On the big table there was a plate of bread and butter, a rack of golden toast, some marmalade, a large pot of tea, and in front of Bessie and myself, a generous plateful of pink curling bacon and two fresh eggs fried to perfection. I fell upon it like a hungry dog, trying not to look at Mrs Black, who sat opposite pecking at a strip of dry toast and sipping black coffee. Once, when I sneaked a look at her I caught an expression of undisguised envy on her face which puzzled me. As I looked back at my plate she picked up her coffee and the morning paper and without a word left us. My relief as she departed was enormous.

Bessie's dark eyes flashed angrily. She picked up the teapot, refilled our cups, and helped herself to more toast which she lavishly covered in marmalade. Whispering, I asked Bessie why Mrs Black had cooked such a good breakfast but had not eaten it herself.

Bessie snorted derisively. 'She wants to stay slim. But she wouldn't have to worry about her weight if she had to work like us.'

She bit into the toast with a vicious little snap and pushed the marmalade towards me.

'Eat all you can! It's good grub here, the only thing which keeps me here. I work like a horse, so she feeds me like one!'

It certainly was good grub. To give her due credit, Mrs Black was a splendid cook and was very generous with the meals. But she made sure she got her pound of flesh. She believed in keeping everything in sparkling order, was a perfectionist down to the last detail. She made life hell for those under her thumb and was a slave-driver of the worst kind.

The Queen's was not a large hotel by any means, there were only five bedrooms upstairs, a bathroom and her private sitting-room. A quaint winding staircase led down to the front bar-room and the snug, and another led down to the 'farm' kitchen that I had just cleaned. Then there was the scullery and pantry and the working kitchen leading into the L-shaped extension which was the tea-room, and its toilet rooms. Bessie did all this work on her own every day under the gimlet eye of Mrs Black, who had spent a small fortune on antiques. It had to be one hundred per cent perfect.

Katie's 2005 return to the Queen's Arms.

It was sheer hell in the afternoon when people began rolling up for afternoon teas. Bessie, resplendent in black and white, face bathed in sweat and breathing heavily, rushed in and out with loaded trays from the tea-room. Mrs Black, white starched overall rustling ominously, stood by the large table cutting piles of teacakes. I stood behind her dithering. Somehow that starched overall frightened me to death as though it emphasised her authority over me. I hated standing so close to her. I had to take the teacakes and toast them on a long fork over the fire of the big range, and pass them over for her to butter. But I shook so much I was either burning the teacakes, or losing them in the flames, earning me the wrath of Mrs Black. I was utterly unnerved in her presence.

When I stood for a moment, uncertain what to do next, she snatched the fork out of my hand and pushed me to the sink to tackle the piles of dishes Bessie was bringing in from the tea-room. She seemed to have overlooked the fact that I was only thirteen years old, had never worked before, and presumed I was born with a prior knowledge of hotel work, and of her hotel in particular.

By six o'clock I felt lifeless and dull, going through the motions of helping Bessie with the piles of washing-up from the tea-room, too tired even to think. Mrs Black prepared some plates of a delicious ham salad, to have with bread and butter followed by cake, for our tea. As usual she ate very little, and when her husband finished his meal, they left us, and went to open the bar. I revived a little after Bessie poured me a second cup of tea, and began to enjoy the meal more now that Mrs Black was no longer sitting facing me, pushing a bit of lettuce around her plate.

Saturday night was busy in the pub, with the usual farmers and village people in the big 'farm' kitchen with their noisy game of darts. Drinks were also served in the tea-room but at a higher price, for people who just wanted a quiet evening out. Mr and Mrs Black served in the bar-rooms, but Bessie had to rush through from there carrying trays of drinks to the tea-room, while I sat listlessly cleaning silver.

When I finally opened the stair door, to climb upstairs to bed, I tried not to look at the mess the farm lads were making in that charming room, which I would have to clean up again in the morning.

Sunday was the same routine, being wakened at five in the morning by Bessie, sharing that welcome pot of tea, beginning the whole remorseless grind all over again. I tried to do my best and dreaded the clock striking eight which signalled Mrs Black bouncing down on me finding fault with everything. I hated the way the black-lead got into my nails, and how my hands were becoming roughened and refused to get clean no matter how hard I scrubbed them.

I had no idea that this is what the world of work could be like. This was not just work, but sheer, relentless drudgery. How I got through the rest of that day I don't know, for I ached all over. The only respite from it was when I sat down to meals.

In the afternoon the tearoom was busy again with Bessie darting in and out, with loaded trays, run off her feet. I don't know how she did it after a morning of heavy cleaning jobs.

When the tea-room finally became empty of customers, Mrs Black told Bessie to make us some tea, while she went upstairs for a rest before opening the bar. We sat down to ham sandwiches, toasted teacakes and jam, with homemade cake to follow, and three welcome cups of tea. After we had finished the washing up and silver-cleaning, Bessie brought over the coronation mug and drew out some three-penny pieces which she pressed into my hand. I almost burst into tears when she told me kindly, 'Despite the Missis raving at you all the time, I think you have worked hard. You are only a schoolkid after all. You deserve some thanks, as well as a few tips from me!'

Without doubt it had been the most harrowing weekend of my young life. I was learning one of life's hardest lessons. If a job was worth doing, it was worth doing well – skimping a job brought no satisfaction. Young as I was, I was able to understand that. But what I couldn't understand was why Mrs Black thought it necessary to bully me into learning. There was never a word of praise or encouragement from her, such as the teachers at school would give, and which Bessie also gave when I had finished a job.

Bessie was the only one who showed she cared about me as a person, and I warmed to her kindness even more when she gave me 3s out of those hard-earned tips. Mrs Black, who had no children of her own, seemed to regard me as nothing more than a slave.

I almost swooned with happiness as well as weariness, when my father arrived later to take me home. I saw Mrs Black chatting to him for a few minutes and slipping a coin into his hand. No doubt it was the 2s paid for my weekend of slavery, which I had hoped to save for Guide meetings. But I had three precious shillings from Bessie which meant more to me than the two Mrs Black gave my father. When we reached home, Mam plied me with eager questions which I was too tired to answer. All I wanted was the sheer bliss of falling into the familiar lumpy bed between my two younger sisters and forgetting about the drudgery I had been apprenticed to. Before I slipped into innocent slumber my father's voice drifted into my consciousness.

'She said there's a job for her when she leaves school.'

My childhood had ended.

Chapter Fourteen

KATIE'S WAR AND THE STEEL GIRLS' STRIKE

When the Second World War broke out in September 1939, I was going on nineteen. My home-town of Barrow was dominated by the huge shipbuilding firm of Vickers-Armstrong who were busy fulfilling orders from the Admiralty for ships, guns and aircraft parts. A small firm, Barrow Haematite Steel Works, were producing steel, having a large order in hand for railway lines for China.

I married in April 1940, a couple of weeks before Dunkirk, and was living in a fourth-floor flat in Barrow Island overlooking the shipyard stocks where I could see an aircraft carrier taking shape. I had to learn to live with the constant hammering that went on day and night from the riveters who were piecing the plates of the battleships together.

Above us, the giant silver bodies of the barrage balloon floated gently in the breeze, protecting the shipyard from low-flying aircraft, and no doubt protecting the tenement flats as well. The ever-present sight of these balloons glinting reassuringly overhead were a comfort to some people, while others wondered uneasily if they would attract the bombers.

In 1941 the government brought in a Compulsory Works Order which enabled them to call up married women who had no children, to fill the gaps in manpower which had taken place when workmen had been called up for the armed forces. Many of these women were housewives struggling along on their husband's Army allotment allowance, so were glad of the chance to earn some money.

I was twenty years old when I received an order to report for war work. To my dismay it was not at Vickers, which was only five minutes'

The buildings in Barrow where Katie made her first home as a newlywed.

walk away, but to Barrow Steelworks on the north side of the town. It was a cold March day when I joined a crowd of young girls who were also making their way along Duke Street, Hindpool, towards the grimy ore-stained gates of the steelworks. We were all strangers thrown together by the maelstrom of war.

I've never forgotten that day, my intense disappointment at not being called in to work at Vickers but to this bleak, grimy place. Or the groans of dismay from the other girls, when we entered those stained gates. Before us was a wide yard criss-crossed with railway lines and we paused to gaze morosely at a line of stained trucks being shunted slowly along. The keen north-easterly wind whipped up a cloud of dust that sent stinging needles of grit into our faces, making us all shriek and cling on to our headscarves.

Ahead of us lay a large corrugated iron building. To its left were glimpses of the sullen grey water of Walney Channel. Shivering, the girls crowded together in a disconsolate huddle. No-one wanted to go any further and they stood there moaning about the war and their lot in it. I shouted above the wind, 'It's no good standing here grousing! Where's your Dunkirk spirit? Let's go inside, it's bound to be warmer in there!'

We entered the gloom of the steel-rolling mill, and were met by Bill Webster, the charge-hand, a sturdily built man of about fifty. He had the red ore-stained face of all steelworkers, and was clad in ore-stained overalls. Some distance behind him hovered Dick Stainton, the foreman, who didn't seem at all happy at the sight of young girls in his workplace. Indeed it wasn't the sort of place I wanted to be in. The air in the mill was so filled with iron-ore dust I could taste it, and the floor was littered with all kinds of discarded metal, rusty iron chains, and odd bits of broken tools, hazards for the unwary.

After Bill had introduced himself and Mr Stainton, we followed him slowly along the mill, listening as he pointed to the huge presses and rollers set in the floor, the seats in little enclosures where young lads sat waiting to operate the rollers, the job which awaited us. Up above, a man in a crane controlled the giant presses.

A blast of white heat that travelled the entire length of the mill heralded the opening of the furnace and the birth of a fiercely glowing white-hot ingot of new steel. This was immediately grappled by the waiting pitch-forks of the furnacemen. Stripped to the waist, muscles rippling, bodies streaming with sweat, they skilfully manoeuvred the awesome monster onto the first set of rollers, quickly moved back, and each began wiping their glistening bodies with a vast handkerchief.

The first huge press was turning now, ready for the fat ingot as it slithered along the clattering rollers showering angry sparks that danced like fireflies in the gloom. Upon reaching the first giant press which squeezed it as effortlessly as though it was butter, it came out the other side in the same way as washing comes out of a mangle, only with many tons more pressure. The man in the crane above watched carefully as, cooling rapidly and changing shape, the steel emerged and dropped on to the next set of rollers, now operated by the lads in the enclosures.

This procedure was repeated in each section of presses and rollers along the full length of the mill, until the ingot became longer and thinner and shaped like a railway line. Finally at the end of this operation, the rail had its jagged ends trimmed neatly by the lad in charge of the billet shears, from where it clattered away to cool and be stored ready for loading onto trucks.

Standing well back we had witnessed the entire shaping of a steel railway line from a huge ingot of white glowing steel. The girls, showing little enthusiasm for their forth-coming job, began to pull their coats tightly about them and stood shivering. My own coat was the worse for wear, and I could certainly feel the draughts blowing in the many gaps of the corrugated iron walls.

'Is it always as cold as this, after the steel has passed, Mr Webster?' I asked him, deciding to be spokeswoman for the dispirited girls. He turned to me relieved that someone was showing some kind of interest, and smiled in friendly fashion.

'I'm afraid so. The job isn't hard, but it gets as hot as hell when the steel comes out of the furnace, but after it has passed, it's so draughty in here we all feel cold. So it's absolutely crucial that you keep your coats hanging on the back of your chair, and put them on like the lads are doing now.'

'If it's this cold perhaps we should keep them on all the time!' One girl insisted loudly. Bill Webster turned to her and shook his head.

'No! I'm afraid that wouldn't do at all. After all the sweating you could catch a chill, unless you put your coat on afterwards.'

We began following Mr Webster away from the mill to where he said there was a canteen. Some of the girls perked up at the thought, expecting there would be a cup of tea with some food, but it was only a small dingy room containing a long table with forms to sit on, while on the green-painted wall was a hot water geyser from which tea could be brewed. Some of the girls sat down on the forms and rested their elbows on the table waiting for Mr Webster to speak.

When one girl opened the only cupboard to find it empty, Mr Webster said apologetically, 'It's not much of a canteen, I'm afraid, so you'll have to bring your own sandwiches, tea, and a mug to drink out of.'

Katie aged nineteen with her twenty-eight-year-old husband Laurence in Barrow.

He nodded towards another door. 'But at least you have some new toilets and wash basins, better than what the men have got.'

He sat down for a moment on the end of one of the forms and surveyed us all thoughtfully. 'Don't look so down-hearted, girls. It all seems a bit strange now, but you will be doing an important job, helping the war effort. The young lads out there will show you tomorrow how to work the levers to set the rollers in motion and be with you for a couple of days until you get the hang of it. After that they'll be on their way to an Army training camp.'

The girls glanced at one another, and one said bitterly, 'I wanted to join the ATS, but my mother wouldn't allow it. I don't know what she'll say when I tell her what a dump I'm going to be working in. I'm sure the shipyard would be better than this!'

The other girls agreed heartily. 'Yes! We would have preferred the shipyard too.'

One girl glanced hopefully across at Mr Webster. 'I don't suppose there's a chance we could go there instead, is there?'

Bill Webster shook his head, 'No. It's up to the Ministry of Labour, not us. We have to take the workers they send us. But I'm sure you girls will be fine once you settle in. You have been told its shift work? 7.00 a.m. to 3.00 p.m., 3.00 p.m. to 11.00 p.m. And don't forget to keep your coat on the back of your chair. There will be plenty of breaks, between the furnace's openings, three of them official tea breaks in this canteen, so remember to bring some tea and food.'

When the girls nodded glumly, he rose from his seat, gave us all a friendly smile, and said, 'I'll see you all tomorrow. And do remember to wear sensible shoes and a boiler suit.'

The next few days, a girl called Violet paired with me as two lads of about nineteen, Jack and Tom, showed us how easy it was to work the rollers, always keeping an eye on the ingot as it came through the pressing, to make sure it dropped safely onto the rollers which we operated, before sending it to the next pressing. The job was as Bill Webster said, not a hard one, but it was *so* boring. The worst part though, was the blast of heat followed by the cold draughts and the shivers if we didn't put our coats on as soon as the ingot clattered away to the next pressing.

In the canteen for tea breaks we had made use of the cupboard to hold our mugs, and a large teapot we had bought in the market quite cheaply, by clubbing together a few pence each, and took it in turns to bring in a precious packet of tea, which of course was rationed, and a bottle of milk. The hot water geyser was very efficient and we looked forward to that mug of tea. We found it better though, to go in the washroom first and rinse our mouths out before drinking our tea.

We were all getting to know each other by name, and during the next few weeks those tea breaks in the canteen became the place for us all to air our grievances. At first when we saw how the iron-ore reddened our faces and hands, even creeping down our neck to our brassière, we giggled and laughed saying we looked like Red Indian squaws. But we soon found it was no laughing matter. Washing it off wasn't easy, and the scrubbing of the wretched boiler suit each week was a chore none of us enjoyed.

None of us liked the two shifts, though the morning one finishing at 3.00 p.m. had some of the afternoon remaining, which was far, far better than starting at 3.00 p.m. and finishing at 11.00 p.m. We all dreaded having to struggle home in the blackout with the ever-present fear that the air-raid siren might blare out and a raid begin. We all would have preferred a straight day like the shipyard, starting 7.30 a.m. to 5.30 p.m. with the lunch hour at 12.00 when the shipyard buzzer blew, until 1.00 p.m. when it blew again to signal a return to work.

More and more we compared our places of work to those women who had been lucky enough to be called up for Vickers shipyard. We envied the girls who were learning to work lathes and milling machines in the West Shop, which was five minutes' walk from my flat, and would have been ideal for me.

Our bitterest grievance, however, was over the poor wages we received, 17s per week, compared to shipyard girls earning £3 or £4, and the chance to earn a bonus, and the fact their work was cleaner and they had better hours! We felt we were being exploited for the steel company's profits. Especially when, a few weeks later Bill Webster told us a steel order had been completed ahead of time.

'You all have fitted in well, girls, you can go home pleased,' he said.

At tea break time we were all very angry as we discussed what he'd said.

'We helped to get that order out, so we should get a bonus, like the shipyard girls, shouldn't we?' Vera shouted slapping her hand down on the table. We all agreed and felt more than ever that we were being exploited. 'I think it's about time we wrote to the managers with our complaints, Vera,' I suggested firmly.

'Would you do it, Katie? I'm not much good at writing letters. Apart from those I send to John,' Vera added, giggling.

At home that night I wrote the letter detailing our grievances, and took it to work the next day. One by one the girls read it, and without my even asking, they all wrote their names under mine. We were solid. At tea break I took it up to the office and handed it to a clerk.

When three weeks went by without receiving any acknowledgement, I marched up to the office and saw the same clerk. I asked him why we hadn't had any reply, but all I got was a brusque, 'Get back to your work!'

Before I could reply he slammed the window down and turned back to his desk. I was absolutely furious. I hurried back to the canteen as fast as I could as our tea break was almost over.

Once inside the door I banged it shut then drew the bolt across. The girls who had risen from the table ready to go back into the mill stared open-mouthed.

'What happened?' asked Vera, and her mate, May asked, 'Why have you bolted the door, Katie?'

'We're on strike!' I exclaimed.

'But how do we go about it?' someone asked as they all began to look excited.

I faced them calmly, my anger leaving me but a firm resolve taking its place. I told them indignantly, 'That snooty little clerk up there ordered me back to work as though I was dirt and he was the big boss himself! So now we'll wait and see what has happened to our letter. I wonder if he read it and destroyed it. If so I'll damn well write another one!'

'What a damned cheek! That's if he did!' Red-haired Vera sat down again and lit a cigarette.

'We might as well have another five minutes and see what happens.'

The girls relaxed and Sheila and Dolly sat down again as well. My mate Violet said to me, 'Come over and sit down, you haven't even had your tea yet.'

The tea was still hot enough to enjoy, so I sat down and began to drink it, wondering to myself what the outcome of my actions would be. We didn't have long to wait. Heavy footsteps sounded outside, and fists began to hammer at the door.

'Open this door at once! What the hell are you playing at?'

It was Dick Stainton, the foreman, and Bill Webster.

We all shouted in unison, 'We're on strike!'

'Like hell you are! The furnace is waiting to open!' Stainton was furious. We heard him talking to Bill, then rushing away. Bill hammered on the door again, and shouted for us to come out.

'Come on girls. Dick has gone for the boss.'

'Good!' I shouted. 'He's the one we want to see!'

This is what I hoped would happen. Stainton arrived back with one of the bosses and they began hammering on the door again. We all rushed to the door to listen as the boss called in a cold hard voice, 'If you come out NOW and get that steel rolling, we'll discuss your letter at three o'clock.'

With that I unbolted and opened the door without hesitation, and the six of us walked out heads held high. Stainton and the boss glared at us red-faced with anger.

When we arrived back at our places all the furnacemen and the crane driver began cheering, whistling, and clapping. The furnace opened its gaping hot mouth, the huge ingot slid out and the steel began to roll once more.

At three o'clock I walked calmly over to the office and the other girls went over to speak to the afternoon shift who were just clocking in. The snooty clerk led me up to the boss's office, knocked on the door, and left me without a word. I felt sure he knew everything that was going on.

I walked in and found myself facing the boss across a huge desk. Mr H, minus his black bowler hat, scowled, banged his red fist on the desk, and promptly launched into a tirade about the seriousness of trying to create an unofficial strike in wartime, the disruption of steel production and so on. It was tantamount to treason, I was letting the country down, and endangering the lives of the armed forces. I felt I was being read the Riot Act and he was trying to humiliate me. It was all rubbish! I wasn't doing anything of the kind. I was just making a stand for the right to be heard.

When he paused for breath he reached across his desk for a folder and withdrew some official-looking papers. Rustling them importantly, he read out an agreement which stated wages would be reviewed every six months depending on production levels achieved. It had been decided to award the women a 10s a week rise, and the men £1 a week rise.

I was triumphant, and it showed on my delighted face. He shot me a steely glance from under bushy eyebrows and demanded, 'Was it you who wrote the letter?'

'Yes! But we were all in agreement.'

He wrote something on a notepad, and gave me a curt nod of dismissal.

A fortnight later back again on the morning shift, I missed the bus and was late arriving for work. I found the clocking-in office closed which meant I had to go around the corner to the main office and knock on the window. The snooty clerk appeared, opened the window slapped my wages and stamp cards at me and snarled, 'You're sacked!'

It was a shock and I felt they were making an example of me to deter anyone else from taking such action in the future. But I was still convinced that I had done the right thing, to strike while the steel was hot.

Chapter Fifteen

A NEW LIFE

When triumph in the Second World War finally came in 1945, shattered cities like London, Coventry, Exeter, Birmingham, Liverpool and Manchester, and towns like Barrow, heaved a sigh of relief and waited for the fruits of victory. But they never came. Of course it was illogical of people to expect an immediate return to peacetime living after six years of war, but it was a natural longing after such privations. People became angry that rationing was to continue for another ten years. To make matters worse, news came in that people in Holland, Germany and the Channel Islands were starving, and food was being airlifted to them. They didn't begrudge food going to Holland and the Channel Islands because they had suffered German occupation, but there was a lot of bitter resentment about feeding Germans who had supported Hitler's Nazi regime so avidly, and many felt the food shortage in Britain was because of this drain on its resources.

Barrow Council was slow in removing derelict houses and beginning a new housing programme. Women who had helped the war effort were dismayed at being laid off by Vickers, and felt the loss of their wages acutely. And worse still, many found that their demobbed husbands were unable to find jobs.

The fact was, of course, that Vickers couldn't return to their peacetime role of shipbuilder overnight and start to build ocean liners. Neither were there any orders coming from the Admiralty for naval ships, in spite of the fact that many of their former warships lay at the bottom of the sea as a result of the war.

People became disillusioned with what they saw as an empty victory, and many with memories of their childhood in the Depression feared for the future. They saw a Britain tied down with a financial war debt to America and felt they themselves would be kept down for years because Barrow and the whole of Britain was in a mess.

In 1948 an Agreement had been reached between Britain and Australia to provide £10 assisted passages for British families who wished to try to make a new life for themselves Down Under. Posters appeared in the labour exchanges extolling the virtues of life in Australia working in the sunshine, and encouraging people to apply for an Assisted Passage from Australia House in London.

In Barrow many people who were enduring unemployment and living in cramped accommodation with relatives, saw this as the answer to their problems. For not only were these cheap fares offered, there was also accommodation available in migrant hostels that were situated around most of the big cities in Australia. All of this information was contained in little booklets sent from Australia House to those who had applied for assisted passages. Then followed interviews and medicals, which if proved successful meant applicants would be offered assisted passages as soon as a ship was allocated.

It was in a cold, bleak January 1954 that a brown envelope fell on the doormat. Moving quickly I stooped down and picking it up turned it over to see what it was. In the left-hand corner it said, 'Australia House, The Strand, LONDON'. Before I had become pregnant with my youngest, I had tried desperately to find work myself. As well as trying for a job at Barrow's laundry I had also tried to get a job as a bus conductress. But it was no use; they only took single girls. On one of my frequent visits to the labour exchange I had seen a huge poster inviting people to apply for emigration to Australia. I scribbled down the address and wrote to it as soon as I got home.

Now the reply was here. The letter contained an application form for assisted passages, plus little booklets extolling the virtues of living and working in Australia, and details of migrant hostel accommodation for families. I filled it in and persuaded my husband to sign it. Afterwards I read the little booklets over and over and swelling with enthusiasm for this new life that was beckoning, I related it all to my husband, who as usual was out of work. I stressed upon him the employment opportunities that we would both have.

My enthusiasm for what I considered to be the door of opportunity carried me through the hardship of my husband's continuing unemployment, and I began watching anxiously for the postman every day. When it came a fortnight later, the reply had been disappointing to say the least. There was an urgent need for skilled artisan tradesmen. Out-of-work lorry and crane drivers were classed as unskilled workers and were not needed. However, the end of the letter stated that the application would be kept on file. This tiny crumb of hope had been enough encouragement for me to keep sending polite letters of enquiry two or three times a year. They answered in less than a month, but the reply was always the same: unfortunately, no assisted passage could be offered as yet.

On that bleak January day in 1954 when I felt we had touched rock bottom, I had no reason to believe the reply would be any different to the dozen others that had come over the three years of writing. I took the letter into the kitchen, lit the gas, and pulled the pan of porridge onto the hob.

I blinked and read the message three times before letting out a little scream and rushing up the stairs. 'We can go!' I shouted. I was out of breath, my throat dry the words coming out in a babble of excitement. 'It s only ten pounds each, and the kids go for free!'

My husband, out of bed at last and half-dressed, snorted, 'What are you on about?'

I waved the letter at him 'AUSTRALIA! Where do you think? Isn't it wonderful news?'

'But I don't want to go to bloody Australia. I'll be alright here as soon as I get another driving job.'

Some of my excitement drained away. 'But you never go out to look for it. Besides, you could take anything until a driving job came your way, but all you do is lie in bed!'

Deep down he knew this to be the case and that going to Australia would solve all manner of problems in one fell swoop. The children would be happier there too.

Katie's family Down Under. Standing, left to right, are husband Laurence, Katie and their eldest son Terry. Seated are Cary, Robin and Glenis.

A New Life

In June 1954 my family and I sailed to Australia and had such an adventure with so many new sounds and sights of the great outdoors, it was a wonderful opportunity to build a new life. But I never forgot Walney Island and my childhood. Despite the sound of the train which sped us away to the port town of Southampton that seemed to echo 'you'll never get back, you'll never get back', I did return later to walk those stony shores once more.

Other titles published by The History Press

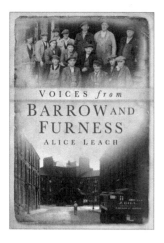

Voices from Barrow and Furness
ALICE LEACH

Barrow-in-Furness grew from a tiny hamlet into the largest iron and steel centre in the world, as well as a major shipbuilding centre, in just forty years. *Voices from Barrow and Furness* draws together memories of life on the Furness peninsula – in Barrow itself, and Dalton and Askham, as well as the villages – from a wide range of people who have fascinating tales to tell, including shopkeepers, an MP, a vicar, an undertaker, a zookeeper and a midwife, to name just a few. The book is also illustrated with a wonderful selection of photographs that capture the spirit of this unique area over the past hundred years or so.

978 0 7509 4743 5

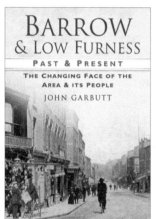

Barrow & Low Furness Past & Present
JOHN GARBUTT

Barrow & Low Furness Past & Present gives a fascinating insight into the dramatic changes that have taken place in the town and surrounding area during the twentieth century, recalling houses and public buildings, shops, factories and pubs that have vanished or have been changed almost beyond recognition. Drawing on detailed local knowledge of the community, John Garbutt has combined a remarkable selection of archive photographs with modern views of the same scenes in order to record the transformation that has occurred. The book will add to the knowledge, appreciation and enjoyment of all those who take an interest in this historic town.

978 0 7509 4982 8

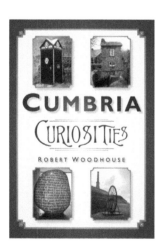

Cumbria Curiosities
ROBERT WOODHOUSE

Cumbria Curiosities brings together a series of unusual, intriguing and extraordinary buildings, structures, incidents and people from all parts of the county. Included in these pages are the Fairy Steps of Beetham Fell; Bonnie Prince Charlie's Chimney; schoolboy graffiti by William Wordsworth at Hawkshead; a hilltop tower at Hampsfell which has poetic advice for travellers; and the world-famous gurning competition at Egremont. As well as these fascinating relics from Cumbria's industrial, ecclesiastical and military past are curious customs at locations ranging from the Irish Sea, to the dramatic peaks of the Lake District and the fertile lowland areas.

978 0 7509 5078 7

Visit our website and discover thousands of other History Press books.
www.thehistorypress.co.uk